JESUS COLORED GLASSES

**Seeing Our Worth And Value
In A World That Doesn't**

TODD JONES

Loganville, Georgia

Copyright © 2018 TODD JONES

All rights are reserved. No part of this publication can be reproduced or copied in any way without the expressed written consent of 228 Publishers and the author. This book was written, printed, and designed in the United States of America.

ISBN: 0-9984876-5-1
ISBN-13: 978-0-9984876-5-6

All Scripture quotations, unless otherwise indicated, are taken from the Holy Bible, New International Version®, NIV®. Copyright ©1973, 1978, 1984, 2011 by Biblica, Inc.™ Used by permission of Zondervan. All rights reserved worldwide. www.zondervan.com The "NIV" and "New International Version" are trademarks registered in the United States Patent and Trademark Office by Biblica, Inc.™

Scripture quotations marked (NLT) are taken from the Holy Bible, New Living Translation, copyright ©1996, 2004, 2015 by Tyndale House Foundation. Used by permission of Tyndale House Publishers, Inc., Carol Stream, Illinois 60188. All rights reserved.

228 Publishers
Loganville, Georgia
www.228Publishers.com

228 Publishers is a Division of Ministry Bubble LLC
228 Publishers President and Publisher: Anne Snyder
Cover and Layout Design: Chase Snyder

Copies of this book are available to churches, schools, and small groups at a significant quantity discount. For more details, go to **www.228Publishers.com**.

TABLE OF CONTENTS

	Introduction	1
1	The Mess	3
2	Why Don't I Feel Amazing?	11
3	Jesus-Colored Glasses	19
4	Created	27
5	Redeemed	35
6	Adopted	45
7	Forgiveness	55
8	The Void	67
9	Worry	79
10	The Right View	87
11	Labels	93
12	Viewing Others	101
13	Conquerors	113
14	Getting Real	123
15	The Right View Every Day	135
	About The Author	147

Introduction

It is no secret that living in our world is not easy. We are all – no matter our age or season of life – constantly told how to look, how to act, and what to do to be accepted by others. We are pulled in so many different directions that it is hard to figure out who we are and even harder to be OK with it.

We may at times feel worthless, small, unimportant, insignificant, and as if everyone else sees that too. It's very easy to feel like we can never measure up to the standards we are held to – standards whose origins we are not quite sure of but definitely feel the effects of. Oftentimes when we try our hardest to fit in, be cool, and do the "right" things, it just doesn't work.

Subconsciously, we ask ourselves these questions: *Who am I? What defines me? How do I fit in? Do I need to change?*

These are all valid questions, and they have answers. Throughout this book I will shed some light on these questions and offer an antidote to the way we typically see ourselves. I plan to turn your questions and doubts into triumphs and confidence. When you discover who you were created to be and see yourself the correct way (the way Jesus sees you), it will change everything!

CHAPTER 1
THE MESS

The Mess

We live in a messed up world. We all experience this mess in one way or another. If you don't believe me, just turn on the news and it will become abundantly clear there is a major mess. It seems as if there is another mass murder, public shooting, or high-profile crime every single day. People find so many different reasons to hate one another, whether it is about race, religion, politics, or because they simply don't like what someone else did. It seems as if love has left the building.

I have seen the mess around me personally in so many different ways just in this last year. It becomes so real and vividly clear when it happens in your city, to your friends, or to you personally. Recently, a young man walked into the mall closest to my house with a gun and opened fire. He shot six people, escaped, and hid for three days before he was apprehended. This year I have experienced the sudden death of a dear friend from unforeseen health issues, watched friends leave their entire families behind, and had family members diagnosed with terminal illnesses. It is one thing to see the mess from afar, but to experience it personally and in your own backyard hits you hard.

A Messy World

I think we would all agree that things are broken and people are too. I know I feel broken at times, like things about me just aren't right, like I am not good enough. I am insecure and self-conscious about my looks, my actions, how I am performing, and whether or not people like me. The media, celebrities, and people we meet all tell us there are standards we must meet and then remind us that we don't meet them. We are constantly told by other flawed people that we are flawed. How does that even make sense?

Really, think about it. Other flawed people set a standard of how we should look, how we should act, and who we should be. Then they judge us by our flaws and failures to meet that standard. There is something wrong with the system.

The world we live in is a mess, and its effects spill over into our lives. The way we view ourselves is a direct reflection of the fallen and messed up world in which we live. If we are real about how we actually feel, most of us don't feel amazing about ourselves. We may be told at times that we are amazing, but the fact of the matter is that is not always how we feel!

Our world is a major mess and even if some people in our lives see us as amazing, the mess seems to overshadow it. Some days when we wake up and look in the mirror, we are shocked by what we see and try desperately to figure out what happened to our faces in the middle of the night. I know I do. We have acne popping up out of nowhere, hair that won't do what it is supposed to, and we can't find any clothes that look good on our bodies.

We feel like we need the makeup counter from the department store to follow us around all day doing touch ups on our faces.

Why do we feel broken, ugly, uncool, not good enough, and simply not right about ourselves? Simply put, we have been messed up.

When God first created each of us, He made us exactly how He wanted us to be – we are each like a masterpiece created by a master painter. But we have been vandalized like a Sharpie taken to a Van Gogh. The original piece of art is absolutely amazing, created perfectly and wonderfully, but somewhere along the way marks were scribbled on the painting, making it difficult to see the original creation. Marks deface God's masterpiece – you – and keep you from seeing the full picture of yourself correctly. Those marks are called sin.

So What Is Sin?

Sin is anything that has been done that goes against God's glorious standard, and its effects are devastating to the world. Since God is perfect, God has a standard of good that requires perfection. Anything less than that standard is called sin, and we live in a world that is fallen and is broken because of sin. God created everything, and He said it was good. He created humans, and He said it was very good. So what happened? The world I see isn't good very often, and the people I see aren't often very good at all. That is because of sin. Sin corrupts all good and has spread to everything. Sin causes death and separation from God. It distorts our perceptions, and it is the reason for the pain and suffering we see in the world.

Sin is like a disease. Take cancer for example. Cancer claims millions of lives per year. You have probably experienced the pain cancer can cause whether it is yourself, a family member, a close friend, or simply a story you heard. Sin is just like a disease, but it is much worse than cancer. It is the worst disease ever because it is what every single person will eventually die from. Of course, death manifests itself differently in everyone, but the root cause of death is sin.

When God spoke creation into existence everything was perfect. Death, pain, and suffering did not exist. The first man and woman, Adam and Eve, literally walked with God. They experienced creation how it was meant to be in the Garden of Eden. One day, Adam and Eve chose to break the only rule God put in place. God allowed them to eat from any tree in the garden except one. (Yep, you guessed it. That is the tree they decided to eat from.) They were tempted and gave in, disobeying God. Like a HAZMAT suit with a tear, in that single act sin entered the perfection God had created and with it pain, suffering, death, and the world we now experience. Death is a consequence of sin in the world and like most diseases, it spreads.

The Bible says in Romans 5 that sin has spread to all people. It is not contagious; you cannot catch it from someone else. You were born with it. You were not born sinful because you had not yet made any choices, but you were born with a proclivity to sin that is impossible to resist. We have all sinned at one time or another in our lives. Sin is the worst type of disease. Not only is it the cause of death, but every person you see is infected with it and has contracted its effects.

Now, I am not calling you, or anyone for that matter, a bad person. I am saying that at one time or another you, I, and everyone has done something that goes against God's standard. Right away you might be thinking, "I am not perfect, but I wouldn't say I deserve death. What is this 'standard' God has for us?"

God's standard is perfection. Perfection doesn't leave any room for error, and anything less than perfection falls short of God's standard. It is like if you were to take a piece of completely white paper – with no dirt or markings – and set it in front of you. The piece of paper is perfectly clean. Then you take a pen and put a little dot right in the center of the paper. That dot might not be big, it might not be bad, but that little dot, no matter how small it is, still messes up the perfection of that paper. The same goes for our sin. Even if we have never killed anyone, stolen anything, or done anything huge, we have still missed the standard of perfection God has set.

The Bible lays out our condition clearly in Romans 3:10 and 23 when it states, "There is no one righteous, not even one. ... All have sinned and fall short of the glory of God."

So, what does that mean for us? Are we just condemned even if what we have done isn't that bad? Yes, that is exactly what it means. The standard is perfection, and since none of us are perfect, we are marked by sin and its effects.

By far the worst effect of sin is that it separates us from God. It keeps us from having a relationship with Him. Along with that separation, we are kept from seeing ourselves clearly. We talked about how God created us amazing and that is how Jesus sees us, but sin prevents us from seeing that. It is exactly like that masterpiece we talked about. A beautiful work of art vandalized and scribbled on with a marker. It is objectively beautiful but we don't see its beauty because all we see are the scribbles all over it. We are not able to see the masterpiece clearly because sin prevents us from seeing it.

The Right Prescription

I think most of us have tried on someone else's glasses at some point, whether it was just being silly with a friend or admiring the style of someone's new pair of specs. Chances are you couldn't see very well when you tried on those glasses; everything was blurry and you probably got a headache because the prescription was wrong. I personally have never needed glasses, so every time I put a pair on that is exactly what I experience. Just like the blur caused by the glasses, sin blurs the way we see ourselves. We are, in a sense, constantly looking through blurry glasses. While we might be able to see a figure in the mirror, we fail to see ourselves clearly. We see and believe what we feel about ourselves and focus on all our shortcomings instead of seeing the real us, the beautiful us, the us that Jesus sees.

CHAPTER 2
WHY DON'T I FEEL AMAZING?

Why Don't I Feel Amazing?

I think we can all agree that there are things about ourselves we don't like when we see our reflection. We could probably write novel-sized lists of the things we would change about ourselves if we could. It doesn't matter how often I am told I have value, it is still hard to believe when I look in the mirror.

It is a well-known fact that plastic surgery is one of the most lucrative occupations around. Plastic surgeons make tons of money and have no shortage of customers because everyone wants to fix something about themselves. People do not like who they are and what they see in the mirror, so they pay someone to change their appearance. These days it seems like you can get anything surgically "fixed" to fit the image you want to project. I even heard an advertisement on the radio recently for a voice lift. Apparently if you don't like your voice you can get a surgery to make you sound more youthful. It's nuts!

When I was in middle school and high school, I remember feeling about an inch tall because of my acne. I felt gross because of it and wanted to hide it as much as I could. I couldn't hide my face, but I could hide the acne on my back. I remember summer after summer sitting by the pool at friends' houses so I wouldn't have to take my shirt off and expose what I hated most about myself. Everyone would be swimming, and I would just be sitting in a chair beside the pool watching everyone else have a blast. When anyone asked, I would just claim that I didn't feel like swimming that day. But in actuality I just didn't like myself, and I didn't want anyone to see me and feel the same.

Being comfortable with yourself is not easy, especially in adolescence. But I learned as I grew up that it is not just adolescence. The acne went away, but then I found other things I didn't like about myself. It seems as if our lives are just a discovery mission to find things that make us feel less than amazing. Once we get over or outgrow one thing, another insecurity comes up. It is a never-ending cycle of finding things we don't like about ourselves.

For me, the next big self-image hurdle appeared as soon as I jumped the previous one. I began losing my hair by the time I was twenty-two. It's really not a big deal at all. Balding happens. But why did it have to happen to me? It was and is just another thing to make me doubt myself and see myself as messed up. I don't feel amazing at all, and that is how most of us see ourselves – as less than amazing.

Not Good Enough

I have always been a driven person who hates to fail. At the age of six I declared to myself that I would be the best T-ball player in the history of baseball. I discovered that if I were able to hit the ball to just the right spot, it would roll right past the left fielder and I could get a home run every time. It was glorious. However, I remember one at-bat where things didn't go as planned. I hit it in the right spot, but somehow the left fielder stopped the ball. I was only able to get a double. I found myself standing on second base crying because it wasn't a home run. How ridiculous is that? Some of the kids on my team couldn't even get a hit, let alone a double, and there I was crying because I failed to hit a home run.

I hold myself to a very high standard and I often find myself measuring my self-worth based on my failures. I feel like I am not good enough if I fail, and my failures haunt me. I think about them often – how I could have done things differently or that I am just not good enough to be doing what I do. My insecurities run deep in both my appearance and my actions – I know I'm not the only one who feels that way. We could be told a thousand times that we are amazing, but the insecurities continue to show themselves.

The Standard Has Been Set For Us

When I was in college, I had the privilege of playing baseball for one of the best programs in the country. We were a very successful, highly respected team and that was no accident; we worked very, very hard for it! In fact, the standards our coach set for us were extremely high and we were expected to meet them both on and off the field. For example, our coach had a special set of rules for our behavior in our classes. We were required to sit in the front row of every class, remove hats, sit up straight, and be active participants. He and his staff would actually poke their heads into our classrooms to check. We were all held to standards we did not choose; they were set for us.

In a much less positive way, the same happens to each of us daily when it comes to the standards society and media have set for us. They tell us what is beautiful and how we should look. Beautiful girls everywhere look in the mirror and think they are ugly or overweight because they measure themselves with that standard. Young men are sold a standard of masculinity and told that if they don't measure up in looks, athletic ability, or popularity they are not valuable to society. We are told we must act a certain way – be funny, carefree, and have tons of friends – and that doing anything contrary to that makes us less valuable. We did not get to choose this standard, and it is not healthy.

Many times we feel as if we do not measure up, like we are failures. But let's pause for a second and ask what we are trying to measure up to and who gets to determine what that standard is. Are we trying to measure up to celebrities whose wealth and perfectly fabricated beauty are so visible to the world? Are we trying to measure up to companies that tell us we need their product in order to matter? Are we trying to measure up to Hollywood's depiction of unrealistic characters living impractical lives that set an expectation of what we should look like, what things we should have, and who we should be?

Fake It And Still Don't Make It

These standards are only intensified by the power of social media. It is a stage on which our looks, our possessions, and our coolness are judged by the world. We are controlled by social media's power to either affirm us or crush us based on how many "likes" we get. We gain so much of our self-image from screens instead of reality. Social media is wrecking us as we try to live up to society's impossible standards.

But the bigger issue comes when we put up a facade to ensure affirmation. It is easy to make up a fantasy world starring us and pass it off as real life. We can simply lie about who we are and hide the real, uncool us by only posting deceiving images and half-truths. Usually it takes ten or twenty selfies before we find the right one but we post it and pretend we just look perfect all the time. We give people what we think they want and the worst part is they like it – I mean, they literally "like" it. We live for those likes. The mere fact that we check for activity every few minutes after posting proves how much the approval means to us. The validation we get on our fake selves is just more reason to hide our imperfections and further promote an unreal image of ourselves. It is fun to create for ourselves what we think people want to see. It is almost like a momentary escape from reality. We can take our boring lives and make them look amazing. But once we log off we are left alone with who we really are in the real world, and it leaves us empty. In many cases, we are left even emptier than before, believing the fake versions of ourselves are more likeable than the real us.

The other danger of social media is that we tend to compare ourselves with others. When we compare other peoples' awesome lives on social media to our not-so-awesome lives, we are comparing apples to oranges because most of what we see is fake. I know many people going through extreme turmoil but by looking at their social media, it appears their lives are perfect.

Someone could be having the worst day of their life – their dog ran away, they broke up with their boyfriend or girlfriend, they lost their job, their life is falling apart – but pull over at the beach on their drive home and take a picture of their toes in the sand, sunset in the background, and caption the picture "just chasing sunsets." Everyone who reads it would think that person has the most magical, wonderful life, but it is so misleading!

We spend our time feeling bad about our lives based on a lie about someone else's life. Social media intensifies our need to meet the completely impossible standards that have been set for us. But that isn't the standard that matters; society and social media do not get to dictate our worth and value. In fact, it has absolutely nothing to do with our worth and value.

It is not easy being alive during a time where media reigns and sets an impossible standard for us to live up to. We spend most of our lives feeling like dirt because of the social pressures we feel and the way we view ourselves. Our self-esteem is gone, our worth is completely missing, and many of us have forgotten we ever had value. But the standard the world has set for us is not the standard we need to judge ourselves by. The world has no authority to say who we are because we have already been told. There is someone who sees us completely differently from how the world sees us and how we see ourselves.

CHAPTER 3
JESUS-COLORED GLASSES

Jesus-Colored Glasses

Have you ever been in love? Maybe you haven't been in love yet, but you have probably had at least one major crush. I remember when my wife and I first started dating. We were young (both 19 years old at the time) and looking good! In fact, she was looking really, really good. When I looked at her, I only saw perfection. We were getting to know each other and discovering things about one another. We were flirting, laughing, and having a great time. I was falling for her fast and hard, and she was falling for me too.

It is said that people in love act as if they are wearing "rose-colored glasses." That phrase describes what happens when you wear glasses with colored lenses. When you look through them, the color of the lenses tints everything you see. People in love tend to see only the rosiest of things about the object of their affection.

When I was dating my wife, it felt like I was seeing cartoon hearts float around her when we hung out. Her quirks were lovable and her flaws were unimportant; perfection was all I could see. To be honest, a decade later I still feel that way when I look at her. Sure, life has happened. Things haven't always been easy. We have added children to the mix, and we have struggled in many ways. But I still wear rose-colored glasses when I look at my wife because I am deeply in love with her. I see her through the lens of my love.

So, why are we talking about rose-colored glasses? Here is the point: You and I must learn to see ourselves the way we are intended to be seen – the way Jesus sees us. We must see ourselves from the point of view from which He sees us and sees the world. We need to put on Jesus-colored glasses so that everything, including the mirror we look into, is tinted by Jesus' perspective.

What Jesus Sees

In the midst of a messy, imperfect world, Jesus sees something completely different than what we see. He doesn't focus on what the world around us focuses on, and He doesn't look at us the way we look at ourselves. We are definitely caught in a major, major mess, but in spite of our grossness and our perception of ourselves, when Jesus looks at us, He sees that we are amazing! He is overwhelmed by our worth, value, and amazingness.

He is omniscient, which means He sees all and knows all. He created everything and so obviously, He understands true beauty. Yet when He looks at us, He sees that we are amazing. In the midst of all your mess and the mess we all live in, when Jesus looks at you that is what He sees! You are amazing, you are special, you are wonderful, and you have incredible value and extreme worth. In fact, the Bible says God thinks about you often and even spent time creating you exactly how He wanted.

Psalm 139:13-18 says:

> You made all the delicate, inner parts of my body and knit me together in my mother's womb. Thank you for making me so wonderfully complex! Your workmanship is marvelous—how well I know it. You watched me as I was being formed in utter seclusion, as I was woven together in the dark of the womb. You saw me before I was born. Every day of my life was recorded in your book. Every moment was laid out before a single day had passed. How precious are your thoughts about me, O God. They cannot be numbered! I can't even count them; they outnumber the grains of sand![1]

His thoughts about you outnumber the grains of sand! I have spent a lot of time at the beach, and one of the things I have learned is that sand gets everywhere. Even when you think you have washed it all away, you find it in random places because there is just so much of it. And I am just talking about the sand that gets on you. Think about all the beaches and deserts and other places that have sand. There is so much sand out there it hurts my brain just a little to think about how many teeny, tiny grains of sand there are. That means He is thinking about you all the time! His thoughts about you are more than the grains of sand, and that is pretty incredible. The God of the universe would not spend that much time thinking about you if you were not extremely valuable to Him.

---

[1] (NLT)

Did you know that when God made the world, He was most proud of making humans? Out of all the beautiful creations – the beaches, the forests, the mountains, the gorgeous and intriguing animals and fish – He was most proud of us. That is incredible. All you have to do is turn on National Geographic to see some of the most incredibly beautiful scenes in nature, all of which were created by God. But in Genesis 1, when God created the universe, He looked at the land He made and said, "It is good." He looked at the solar system, the sun, moon, and stars and said, "It is good." He looked at all the different kinds of animals He made and He said, "It is good." Then God decided to make human beings and when He was finished, He looked at them in Verse 31 of Chapter 1 of Genesis and He said, "That is very good!" God made us, and we are *very good*. You are a masterpiece.

The Greatest Compliment

He sees us as an amazing, wonderful masterpiece. In fact, the Bible even says in Genesis 1:27 that we are created in God's image. Literally the image of God Himself. Do you understand how big of a compliment that is? I don't know about you, but I absolutely love getting compliments.

A few years ago, my first children were born. Because they are twins, my wife and babies needed to stay in the hospital a few days to recover. For security reasons, in order for me to get in and out of that wing of the hospital I had to be buzzed in. I began seeing the same nurses over and over again. One of the nurses who continually unlocked the door for me asked if she knew me from somewhere. I didn't think so but we talked for a moment and figured out I was right, there was probably no way she knew me. The next day, I went to buzz in and that same nurse came up to me exclaiming that she had figured it out. I was really eager to find out who it was and was just hoping it wasn't some old, scary-looking dude. But what she said was very shocking, and made me feel great! She said, "I don't remember his name, but he was just voted the sexiest man alive." I couldn't believe my ears. I thanked her profusely and marched straight into my wife's hospital room to inform her of how lucky she was to have me as a husband! It was an unexpected but awesome compliment, and I remind my wife of it often.

Now, that nurse may have just worked a twenty-four-hour shift and been having trouble seeing, but the compliment still felt great. I love getting compliments because they make me feel good about myself, and I am sure you do as well. Well, God has given us the greatest compliment of all time; He created us in His image. "In the image of God" should speak volumes about who we are and how we are seen. It is a lot like being told we look similar to the sexiest man alive. We are seen as absolutely amazing and were even created by God with that in mind. The artist Himself took time to create us, thinks about us, and gave us the biggest compliment. You must be amazing if those things are true.

In a world that tells us we don't measure up, we often lose sight of who we were created to be. We get caught up in all the mess around us and we begin to use that mess as a filter when we look at ourselves. We struggle immensely to see ourselves the right way, but God sees us in exactly the right way. He sees us as amazing, as people who have extreme worth and value and who were created perfectly, exactly how He wanted! You are amazing, and that is exactly what Jesus sees when He looks at you.

CHAPTER 4
CREATED

Created

When I was in high school, my best friend Matt and I dreamed about owning mini-motorcycles for months. We soaked up every bit of information we could find, watched videos, and even went to the store to drool over them. They were awesome, but two fifteen-year-olds without incomes couldn't afford them. Matt's dad owned a successful flooring company and pitched us a wonderful idea. He would buy the motorcycles in exchange for 120 hours each of labor for his company. We started the next week. It was very hard manual labor in the middle of the blazing Southern California summer. We woke up early on our break to sweat, strain, and work for what we'd dreamed of for so long. We printed pictures of the bikes and taped them where we were working to motivate us. It was the hardest work I'd ever done, but I pushed through. I will never forget the day we picked up the brand new motorcycles. We put in the work and earned what we wanted.

It was a great experience for me as a young man – I learned the value of working for what I desire. It is the epitome of the American dream. If we put in the time and effort doing what we are supposed to, we earn the desired outcome. Most of us are ingrained with this mindset. But this thinking is completely false when it comes to your worth and value. We are constantly looking for ways to earn what we want, but that is not how God works. There is absolutely nothing you can do to earn your value. It already exists. You are already enough.

You are wonderful. You are beautiful. You are important. You are fun. You are talented. You are valuable. You are worthy of being loved.

There is nothing you can do to earn your worth or value. Your value has already been assigned to you – it doesn't come from your parents, friends, teachers, ex, boss, significant other, or anyone or anything else. Your value comes from God, and it was given to you when He created you. Your value was set at creation and sealed by His death and resurrection. There is nothing you can do to earn it. There is no standard you have to meet or live up to in order to earn your worth and value.

The Opinion That Matters

God gave you your value. He knitted you together and purposefully chose what it is that makes you unique. Yes, you have flaws because of sin, but that does not change the value God has given you. You do not have to hit a certain benchmark or achieve something to get your value. What does a masterpiece have to do to have worth? Absolutely nothing. The artist does the work and gives value to the art. The piece of art cannot do anything; it is up to the artist. You are an amazing work of art, and there is nothing you are capable of doing to gain value. It has been there all along.

At times, however, it can be difficult for us to see our value because we are trying to earn it. We place conditions on ourselves that get in the way of seeing what is already there. If we hang out with a certain group of people, then we have value. If we get that job, then we have value. If we have a certain body type, drive a nicer car, are more athletic ... then we have value. But that is completely false. We must stop finding our value in the criteria that we, or the people around us, set.

I know, that is way easier said than done. Growing up, baseball was my life. My performance at each game determined my attitude and mood for the rest of the day and sometimes the next day. If it was a good game, I was happy and fun to be around. If I had a bad game, it was best if everyone stayed away. I think we do the exact same thing with whatever it is we place our worth and value in. If we don't do well in that area, we feel as if we are worthless. In reality, those things have nothing to do with our value because our value is already set. We are already enough.

Jesus is king and ruler over everything, which means His opinion is the only one that counts. We get caught up trying to impress people whose opinions don't matter at all. Jesus is the only one we need to impress. But guess what? We already have! He is already impressed with us. When He looks at us, He sees amazing! He sees wonderful! He sees extreme worth and value, enough worth and value for Him to give His life for you on the cross.

Jesus is able to see through the markings covering the masterpiece. Why? Because He is the artist who created it. He intimately knows every detail, and He loves the masterpiece with all His heart. Jesus loves you in spite of the mess you are in.

Jesus saw your worth and value from the beginning. The Bible says that Jesus was with God in the beginning[2], which means He knows the extreme value that was placed in each one of us. We talked about how in Psalm 139 it says:

> You made all the delicate, inner parts of my body and knit me together in my mother's womb. Thank you for making me so wonderfully complex! Your workmanship is marvelous—how well I know it. You watched me as I was being formed in utter seclusion, as I was woven together in the dark of the womb. You saw me before I was born.[3]

Your value has existed as long as you have, and there is nothing that can be done to convince Jesus of your value. He already knows it!

You are enough because your value is not about what you do – it is about who created and designed you. We are never going to measure up because none of us are perfect. If we place our worth in meeting standards, we will forever see ourselves as failures and losers. There has never been nor will there ever be someone who can do everything right, except Jesus. We have human restrictions, which means none of us will be the best at every sport, get perfect scores on every assignment, or have a flawless appearance. We will always fall short.

That is why it is so important we realize our value is not tied to what we do but rather to whom we belong. If you have placed your faith and trust in Jesus, you belong to

---

[2] John 1:1
[3] Verses 13-16a. (NLT)

Him because He purchased you. We belong to Him, and that simple fact is the reason we are amazing. No one can reach the ridiculous standards we have set for ourselves. Even if someone is the best at sports or academics or looks, they will fail in another area. No one is perfect in all areas, which means they are failures at some. Everyone fails.

At some point, all the things the world says give us our value will go away. Good looks fade, and parts sag, wrinkle, and change. That is just how it is. Our bodies and brains give up, and there will always be someone better than us. So, even if someone is good at sports, there will come a day when their body won't allow it anymore. Things fade and our abilities go away, but who we belong to remains the same. We need to place our value in that truth because it will never change. We are unable to earn it or be enough for it. We already are enough.

Loved

So, what can you do to make God love you? How do you get yourself to belong?

Answer: Nothing. You can't.

You are loved by God because you are you. That is something we struggle with because we don't experience that type of love often. It is foreign in our world and culture. We feel like we have to do something to be worthy of love and praise. God says you are loved because you are you. You cannot be anyone else, and being something other than yourself won't get you love because He loves the real you.

Jesus didn't die for a performance you did. He died for you. God doesn't want fake. He wants you. You are loved exactly how you are. You are enough.

CHAPTER 5
REDEEMED

Redeemed

As first-time parents, my wife and I were blessed with twins. This meant twice the work, and things were pretty crazy at times. I remember one night I was approaching about two hours of sleep when I heard crying. I walked to their room in a zombie-like state expecting to simply put a pacifier back in a mouth, pat a back, or pull a blanket back on. What I was met with was chaos. As soon as I opened the door, I was accosted by some very unhappy screams and a smell that hit me like a ton of bricks. Apparently, one of my babies had gotten sick and it came on strong in the middle of the night. Everything that was supposed to be inside the diaper was outside the diaper. It was everywhere! To make things worse, she had also thrown up everywhere. The kid was covered in poop, the crib was an absolute mess, and her clothes were completely soiled. I know, I have described a beautiful scene for you, and you are completely grossed out right now. So was I! As the type of person who does not like to be dirty at all, I was having trouble even being in the room. It was an absolute, complete disaster. I stood in the middle of the room, fully awake at that point, trying to decide what my first course of action should be. I looked at my daughter, and she looked back at me with pain and confusion in her eyes. She then stretched out her arms for me to pick her up and rescue her. There was nothing beautiful or wonderful about the situation, but I ran over and picked up my little girl and held her close.

It was absolutely disgusting. Despite the mess and smell, I wanted nothing more than to run to my child, whom I deeply love, and hold her in my arms. Why? Because she belongs to me. She is mine, and I love her enough to do what it takes to save her from her situation. And that is exactly what God wants to do with you.

God Loves

In spite of your mess, your sin, and your problems, God wants to save you because He loves you. He has done what it takes to invite you to be a part of His family. You did nothing to deserve this love. There is nothing anyone can do to earn this love. It is a free gift that God has given to everyone. The Bible says in John 3:16, "For God so loved the world that He gave His one and only Son, that whoever believes in Him will not die but have eternal life."

God loves everyone in the world. That means God doesn't care about race, economic status, popularity, body type, looks, or anything else. He loves because that is who He is. In spite of anything you have done or anything that has been done to you. And in spite of what you think about yourself or what people think about you, God loves you!

For some of you, this is weird to hear because you don't feel lovable, and you may never have been told you are loved by anyone. That is the beauty of God's love; it is freely given, pure, and is literally the definition of what love is supposed to be. It feels wonderful! So, how much does He love us?

God loved you enough to send His only son to die for you. We all know the story of Christmas, the night little baby Jesus was born. But most people do not know that the story is way less about a baby and way more about the greatest rescue mission of all time. God sent Jesus to this world to live the life we are unable to live. Jesus grew up in the same world, filled with the same temptations and struggles we face, but He didn't give in to any of them. Jesus lived the perfect life, yet He went to the cross as a sacrifice in our place. He suffered and died for us, and the Bible says God sent Him for that purpose.

That is extreme love, not just fleeting words but a deep, real love. It is one thing to say some words, but we all know words are empty without actions. God took action on that love and His reason for that action was you and all of humankind. He had enough love for you, the way you are, to send Jesus to die for you. You are worth enough for God to give up His son. You are extremely valuable.

This idea became real for me when I became a father and understood a father's love firsthand. It hit me hard – God gave up His son for us. I am sure you are a great person, and I love to help people. But I am telling you right now that if I had to give up my child to save you, I hope your death isn't too painful. Is that too harsh? Honestly, I don't care because that is how much my children mean to me, and that is my exact point. God loved *you* enough to send His son to die so you could be saved. That is extreme love.

The Value Is Determined By The Price Someone Is Willing To Pay

My parents live in Southern California and have a nice-sized backyard with lots of trees and bushes. One type of tree in their yard was this upside-down-octopus-looking thing that looked like it had jumped right out of a Dr. Seuss book. To my family, they were just trees, and not particularly pretty ones at that. One day, the doorbell rang and the man at the door asked if my parents would be willing to sell the trees to him. He went on to explain that he was a movie producer and had been searching all over for that type of tree for a set he was building. My parents really didn't care about the trees and didn't see any value in them, so they were completely astonished when the man offered to pay $1,000 each. They immediately took the offer and were glad they did because they had six of them on their property.

The value of those trees was determined by what someone was willing to pay for them. They were extremely valuable, even if my parents didn't see it. The person who set the value was the guy who was willing to pay such a large amount of money for them.

Jesus determined your value when He was willing to pay the highest price for you. He is the one who paid for you, so He gets to set your value. It doesn't matter what anyone else, including yourself, thinks of your value. The cross is a symbol that carries so much meaning because it doesn't just represent the fact that you are a sinner – it represents your value. When Jesus went to the cross, God determined your value. What He saw in you was someone worth paying the ultimate price for. Too often, we look to other things to see our value when God has already shown us with His actions.

You are worth it. That may be a sentence you have never heard and definitely don't tell yourself, but it is true. Your worth and value were sealed by Jesus hanging on a cross in your place. Not only were you worth God sending His son, but you were also worth Jesus Himself willingly going to the cross. Jesus didn't fight it. He didn't run. He didn't argue. He willingly went to the cross and died for you.

Think about it, Jesus was fully man and fully God. This means Jesus had the full power of God. He could have snapped His fingers and been off that cross in a second. He could have stopped it all, said He'd had enough, and been done at any time. Yet He did not do that, He stayed on the cross and went through with it to the point of death. Why? Because of you. You are worth it. Even if you doubt your worth, Jesus didn't for a second.

He Made A Way

Here is the best part. Not only did Jesus die for you because you are worth it, but His death and sacrifice mean life for you. Jesus died for the sins of the world, for every bad thing that you and I have ever done. He paid the price for our sins. But He didn't stay dead. In Luke 24, the Bible says after being dead for three days, Jesus rose from the dead and in so doing He conquered death and conquered sin so that you and I can be saved.

Jesus died for us, and through His death we have a way to God. You see, God is perfect. Because of His perfection, He cannot be with people who have not lived up to His glorious standard (the standard we talked about earlier). If He did, it would ruin His perfection. But God loved us enough to make a way to be with us, and that way is Jesus.

God willingly sent Jesus to earth for you, and Jesus willingly came to earth for you. God willingly sent Jesus to the cross to pay for you, and Jesus willingly went to the cross for you. He endured pain, humiliation, and the weight of the sins of every single person on the planet. That means God had to turn His back on Jesus in that moment – the worst pain possible. Jesus went through with it for you, to pay your debt and purchase you.

The best part is that after Jesus died and was put in a tomb He didn't stay there. After three days He rose from the dead and in so doing conquered sin, conquered death, and made a clear path to God. The resurrection of Jesus is the declaration of independence for anyone who accepts Him.

All we have to do is accept what Jesus did for us on the cross. Accept His death as the payment for your sin and trust Him with your life. Allow Him to come into your life and be part of everything you do. There is nothing you can do to earn it – it is a free gift. And all you have to do is take it. Once you have accepted His gift as a sacrifice on your behalf, when God looks at you He no longer sees your sin. Instead, He sees Jesus.

It is the most important and most wonderful decision you will ever make. So if you have never made that decision before, do it now. Don't let another day pass without putting your faith and trust in Jesus. No one can make this decision for you. It is completely up to you, and it will change your life forever. If you have more questions, need help, or just want to talk to someone about it, look me up. You'll find all the ways to contact me in the back of this book. I would love to talk to you about how God is working in your life.

CHAPTER 6
ADOPTED

Adopted

Far too often we associate what we do with who we are. Growing up, I found my identity in baseball. It was my life and my purpose. My friends, family, and teachers associated me with baseball, and so did I. Every social gathering I attended, I fielded hours of questions about baseball. It was my interest, so it's what people talked to me about. But more than that, it was who I was, which was completely fine with me because baseball was where I could stand out and be awesome. I felt safe talking about baseball because I could pretend to be modest while subtly bragging the whole time, feeling better and better about myself. I loved it. Putting my worth and value in baseball felt good because I was good at it. The problem came when my playing career ended. From as young as I could remember, my plan had always been to play baseball forever. But that didn't happen. My baseball career came to an end.

We place ourselves in a dangerous situation when we find our worth in our career, friends, activities, or anything else. The reason it is dangerous is because those things come to an end. Eventually they stop, they run out, or we are not capable of keeping up. Then what? Our sense of belonging is gone because we placed it in something that wasn't permanent. Even if I had gone on to play Major League Baseball and had a long career, it would still come to an end at some point. Because of the nature of sports, it probably would have ended by the time I turned 40. I would still have so much life ahead of me, but the thing in which I found my worth and value would be over. We need to place our value in our belonging because that is lasting.

So if you don't belong to the things you do, where do you belong?

Adopted

We all know what adoption is. You probably know someone who is adopted, or maybe you are. Adoption is an idea that is very present and clear in the Bible. It defines our standing with God once we are saved. Through Jesus' death and resurrection, God has adopted us. He has paid our debts and made us part of His family. John 1:12-13 reads, "Yet to all who did receive Him, to those who believed in His name, He gave the right to become children of God—children born not of natural descent, nor of human decision or a husband's will, but born of God." The moment we place our faith and trust in Christ, we are counted as children of God and we get to enjoy the freedoms and privileges that come with that title. As children of God, we are fully His; we belong to Him and we are included in His inheritance. That is where our belonging must come from – not from what we do, but from the One to whom we belong.

The Bible says in Galatians 4:6-7, "Because you are His sons, God sent the Spirit of His Son into our hearts, the Spirit who calls out, 'Abba, Father.' So you are no longer a slave, but God's Child; and since you are His child, God has made you also an heir."

Coaches in every sport encourage their players to forget the name on the back of their jerseys (their own) and focus on the name on the front (their team). The sentiment in this instruction is to get players to place their team above themselves and to start finding their identity in the team and working toward the team's well-being. It is good advice for a sports team and good advice for us. Our team name reads "God's Family." Sometimes the name on the back isn't necessarily our name but rather the activity or situation that we get our identity from. If we focus on the name on the front and forget whatever other names might be on our backs, our lives will change drastically. You have been given your identity in God's family, and that identity cannot be taken from you.

Remember your status in Him and remind yourself that placing your identity in any other thing is not going to work out. Author Henri J.M. Nouwen says in his book *Here and Now: Living in the Spirit*, "Jesus came to announce to us that an identity based on success, popularity and power is a false identity- an illusion! Loudly and clearly he says: 'You are not what the world makes you; but you are children of God.'"[4] You are enough because your value is not about what you do; it is about the One to whom you belong.

Fully Accepted

I have the privilege of having four cousins who are adopted. They are wonderful gifts from God that almost didn't make it into our family. My aunt and uncle

---

[4] Nouwen, Henri J.M. *Here and Now: Living in the Spirit.* (Crossroad Publishing Company, 1994)

adopted each of their children by standing in front of abortion clinics and talking to young ladies who were heading inside. Each baby was destined to have their life ended until my aunt and uncle stepped in and agreed to adopt them into their family. That is exactly what God has done for each of us who has accepted Jesus. We were destined for death because of our sin until God stepped in and paid the price for us by sending Jesus to die in our place. We were adopted into God's family.

My cousins are totally and completely part of our family, and they get all of the benefits of being part of our family. As a part of God's family, we get all the benefits of being His son or daughter. His love for us is unconditional – it's not based on our behavior. We simply receive it because we are a part of His family.

Identified As Family

When I was growing up playing baseball all the time, my parents worked really hard to make sure that my worth, value, and identity were not in baseball. They knew it was a huge part of my life and supported me completely, but they often told me they loved me no matter what. Whether I won or lost, had a great game or a terrible one, they loved me and I knew that. They didn't love me because of baseball. They just loved me. Then, I met my wife and she did the same thing. In fact, she didn't even like baseball. She liked me in spite of baseball. Baseball had nothing to do with the way she saw me or her affection for me. Those were some of the major reasons that when baseball did end for me, I was able to move on. I knew there was more to life and there was more to me.

Over the last few years of my baseball career I began to understand identity, and I discovered my identity didn't need to be in baseball. Baseball was something I did, not who I was. Was it still hard when it was over? Yes! Picture a man in his early twenties crying his eyes out and not even taking his cleats off because he knew it was the last time he would ever do that. That is exactly what happened, and it was extremely difficult. It was the end of a major part of my life, something I had been working on and working toward for most of my existence. But as devastating as it was, my life wasn't over at that point because my identity was no longer placed in that activity. My identity was as a member of God's family.

Jesus Christ loves you because you are His, not because of what you do. In fact, He loves you in spite of what you do. Titus 3:5 says it's not because of the things we do that Jesus loves us, but rather it's because of His mercy. Pastor and author Steven Furtick puts it this way, "And even when you can't seem to get your act together, your identity is secure and completely intact. Because in Christ, who you are matters infinitely more than anything you do or cannot do."[5] Your identity isn't in anything other than Christ, and that is where the firm foundation is found.

Being part of God's family is awesome! We are literally saved from our past and made part of God's family to partake in His inheritance. We are given our identity in Him and are considered full-fledged members of His

---

[5] Furtick, Steven. *Crash the Chatterbox: Hearing God's Voice Above All Others.* (Multnomah Books, 2015) p.27

family. The best part is that because God does not change, His truth and His promises do not change either. This is why an identity as a child of God is permanent – a solid foundation. However, the fact that it is true does not mean we can't forget it. Our adversary as Christians, the devil, is working all the time to make us lose our identity in other things or simply believe the lie that we do not have an identity at all.

You have a wonderful identity. You are part of God's family! We do not need to look any further because nothing else will hold up or last. Our identity in Christ is the only thing that will last and will not change when situations in life change. We must learn to make that our primary source of identity and cling to the fact that we have been purchased with a price and adopted into God's family. When your identity is in Him, it cannot be taken from you by the lies and accusations of the enemy. It is something we need to remind ourselves of daily because, as I am sure you know, it's easy to forget who we belong to.

A Feast Is Waiting

Friends of mine adopted a few kids from an extremely poor area in Africa. They adopted the children over a span of four years, and each child was around seven years old when they were adopted. The parents already had a few children but these additions were given all the same rights as the other family members. They were given their own bedrooms, clothing, toys, and food, just like everyone else. They were treated like any other member of the family because that is who they were. For weeks the adopted children were blown away by the amount of food on the table every night at dinner and ate until they were stuffed. But every night the littlest son snuck out of his bed and went through the trash, picking out scraps of food to hide in his room because he didn't yet understand that his new life was permanent. My friends told me each of the kids went through this phase. Not knowing how long their new life would last, they dug in the trash for scraps. Each one of the children had a feast waiting for them every single day at the table, yet still picked scraps out of the garbage.

It is so sad, but that is exactly what we do. In Christ, we have a feast waiting for us but find ourselves picking out of the garbage. We have been adopted into God's family and given an identity in Him, yet we still turn to other things to place our identities in. God loves you so much and He wants you to turn to Him. You matter deeply to God and you have extreme worth and value because you belong to Him.

So, what is your identity in? Where do you get your worth, value, and acceptance? Is it in Christ or in something else? Think about what you do. Is it simply something you do, or does it define you? Write down some of the places you find your worth and value (AKA your identity). It may be your job, your abilities, your friends, your significant other, or anything else that defines you. Think about it and write it down. Listing where our identities lie is the first step in changing it. We need to learn to place our value in our identity in Christ and not let the world, others, or ourselves dictate who we are.

CHAPTER 7
FORGIVENESS

Forgiveness

Now, it is my hope that each one of us has a desire to move forward in our view of ourselves. Unfortunately, a lot of us are held back from seeing ourselves correctly and are held back in our relationship with Christ as well. One of the biggest factors holding us back is the lack of forgiveness in our lives. When we hold grudges, progress is halted. Our worth and value is clouded because we are holding onto something that was done to us and most likely shaped us into who we are. In order to move forward with our self-image, we need to work on forgiveness.

While training to be a top-level athlete in college and beyond, one of my team's exercises was weight resistance training. We carried extra weight when we did certain activities to increase the level of difficulty. As a result, when the weights were removed, we were stronger. The movements became very easy because we were used to doing them with the weights. You may have done something similar like putting on ankle weights or a weighted vest or simply a backpack full of rocks. These weights make it difficult to move around and complete tasks. However, the weights may be heavy but they are easy to bear because we know we will eventually take them off.

But imagine with me for a moment that you didn't take them off. You wore ankle weights and a backpack full of rocks everywhere you went: to the grocery store, the bathroom, sports practice, work, or parent teacher conferences. I think a few things would happen. First, you would be tired all the time and activities that are normally easy would wear you out quickly. Second, you wouldn't be able to reach your full potential. You simply would not function as well because you would be weighed down.

That is exactly what it is like going through life without forgiveness. Anger is a weight on your life. Its effects are very similar to that of wearing ankle weights and a backpack full of rocks. You will not be able to reach your full potential. Will you be able to go on in life? Sure, you can live your whole life without forgiving someone. But you will continue to hold onto that weight until you choose to forgive. Forgiveness is your decision to give or not, but choosing not to forgive someone leaves you with unnecessary weight. That weight will keep you from reaching your goals.

Author Anne Lamott says it another way in her book *Traveling Mercies: Some Thoughts on Faith* when she says, "In fact, not forgiving is like drinking rat poison and then waiting for the rat to die."[6] That sounds like insanity. It will obviously not hurt the rat, but it will destroy the person who drank it. In the same way, we are the only ones who suffer when we are unable to forgive. The other person is not held back when we hold a grudge, but we most definitely are.

When we hold on to anger, we tie ourselves to what was done to us and allow ourselves to be continually dragged down by it. We enable that person or situation

---

[6] Lamott, Anne. *Traveling Mercies: Some Thoughts on Faith.* (Anchor Books, 1999) p.120

to have power over us. Our self-worth and value are determined by that person rather than by Jesus. If we want to see ourselves the way Jesus sees us, we must first experience the freedom that comes from forgiving others.

I am not going to lie and say forgiveness is easy because it's not. People do terrible things. Maybe it's a father who walked out on your family or a spouse who cheated. Maybe it's someone who molested, raped, or assaulted you. Maybe it's a group of people that pushed you away and bullied you. I don't know who it is for you, and I don't know what was done to you. But I do understand that forgiveness is hard.

I am not going to tell you to just get over it because I know it's not that easy. I've felt pain, and I know forgiving is not an easy thing to do. The pain is real and the feelings you are experiencing are real. They are not something you simply get over. But if you want to move forward and experience all that Christ has for you, you must forgive that person. Only then will they no longer have a hold on your life. Take off the ankle weights and backpack known as anger so you can excel in your relationship with Christ and in your view of yourself.

Forgiveness Brings Freedom

When you forgive, freedom is won and the freedom is not for the person you are forgiving. It is for you. Jesus said He came so we could experience life to the fullest. When we are unable to forgive, we put on weights and limit ourselves. God wants us to experience amazing things, but some of us will never reach those heights because we are held back by anger. When you forgive, you experience freedom.

If you want to start seeing yourself the way Jesus sees you and put on Jesus-colored glasses, then it is essential to forgive those who have wronged you. When you are released from that burden, the true you comes into focus, no longer defined by what happened to you. You are no longer a victim. You are simply you.

If you want to move forward and see yourself correctly, you must let go of what you have been holding onto. Andy Stanley challenges the readers of *Enemies of the Heart: Breaking Free from the Four Emotions That Control You* by asking, "Here's a question every angry man and woman needs to consider: How long are you going to allow people you don't even like — people who are no longer in your life, maybe even people who aren't even alive anymore — to control your life? How long?"[7]

Dropping what you have carried for years is liberating. The burden you have carried around because of what someone else did to you can be stifling. When you make the choice to forgive that person, the hold they have on your life is released. That weight is lifted from your shoulders and you are free to see yourself clearly. You are no longer defined by what was done to you. You are now defined by forgiveness – the forgiveness Christ offers you and the forgiveness you gave.

---

[7] Stanley, Andy. *Enemies of the Heart: Breaking Free from the Four Emotions that Control You.* (Multnomah Books, 2006) p.134

How Do You Forgive?

I get it. Way easier said than done. You may completely understand the need to forgive. But how do you go about doing it, and what does it look like?

Have you ever put together a piece of furniture from IKEA? There are always so many parts and so many steps. Luckily, they include a pretty detailed set of instructions. I am definitely not the most mechanical person out there. In fact, I am terrible at it! My dad can fix or build anything but here I am, trying to fit the square peg in the round hole and not understanding why it doesn't work; those instructions are my only hope. I have to look very carefully at the examples provided if I want to complete the assembly. When I am able to look at the pictures and follow the example, I can actually put the pieces together and make it work. The same applies to forgiveness. It does not come naturally to us, and that is why it is so helpful that we have an example to look at. We can follow God's example to learn how to forgive those who have hurt us.

God forgives us in an amazing way. When you look at the forgiveness He has given us, you see that God forgives us in two clear ways. First, He forgives us *totally* and second, He forgives us *repeatedly*. Totally and repeatedly – that is the example for us to follow.

He totally forgave us. There were no conditional clauses in His forgiveness offer. He didn't forgive you for most of it but still hold onto that one thing you did that was pretty messed up. God totally and completely forgives you. That is exactly how we need to forgive –

totally and completely, as if that person does not owe you anything anymore. Sometimes we hold back or give forgiveness only halfway. This type of forgiveness makes us feel OK while allowing us to hold on to anger at the same time. We must learn to forgive totally just as God forgave us totally.

God also forgives us repeatedly. This is great news for us because we repeatedly commit sins. God's forgiveness continues because we continue to need it. There is never a time that God will not forgive you when you repent.

We must also follow that example and forgive repeatedly. Following God's example looks a little different for us because we are not God. Forgiving repeatedly does not mean staying in abusive situations that require forgiveness for offenses repeated over and over. What I mean by forgiving repeatedly is choosing to let go of your anger repeatedly. Because feelings of pain and hurt tend to creep up often, you have to repeatedly remind yourself to let it go. Every time I recall old pain, I feel the same old emotions creep up. Those feelings have not gone away or disappeared, and so I need to remember how God forgave me – totally and repeatedly. Just because the anger and other emotions associated with the things that happened to you arise does not mean you haven't actually forgiven that person. We are human, so those emotions will continue to exist, and many times they are helpful in keeping us out of potentially bad situations where more pain will occur. But that is why we must remind ourselves of the forgiveness that has taken place and follow God's example in offering forgiveness repeatedly.

I am so grateful for the forgiveness I have been shown by God, and I am also grateful for His example so I can choose to forgive.

Why Do You Need To Forgive?

It would be so much easier if we didn't have to forgive others. Many times we are not the ones who did anything wrong, and those who hurt us often don't ask for our forgiveness.

We forgive because we have been forgiven. That is the nature of forgiveness. If you have experienced God's forgiveness in your life and you fully understand the magnitude of what He has forgiven you for, then you understand why forgiveness is necessary. Does that make it easy? No. But if you have been forgiven, then you need to forgive others. Andy Stanley makes this statement in his book *Enemies of the Heart: Breaking Free from the Four Emotions that Control You,* "In the shadow of my hurt, forgiveness feels like a decision to reward my enemy. But in the shadow of the cross, forgiveness is merely a gift from one undeserving soul to another."[8]

Oftentimes, we think of forgiveness as a good thing, a generally great concept. Most of the time, we encourage others to forgive, but it's a different story when it comes to ourselves. We think forgiveness is a great idea for other people but not for us. Sometimes, we justify our anger by how badly we were treated.

---

[8] Stanley, Andy. *Enemies of the Heart: Breaking Free from the Four Emotions that Control You.* (Multnomah Books, 2006) p.129

Let's look at Jesus as another great example to learn from. During the last twenty-four hours of Jesus' life before His death on the cross, He experienced an extreme amount of pain and suffering, both emotional and physical. Every bit of His pain was caused by people. Jesus was turned over to the authorities by one of His close friends. He was abandoned by the rest of His friends, who bailed when He needed them most. Then His best friend denied three times that he even knew Him! Jesus was beaten over and over again, spit on, and humiliated. He was wronged in every possible way.

Yet as Jesus hung on the cross, in the middle of all of His pain and suffering, He chose to forgive. Bloodied, beaten, and almost dead, He asked God to forgive them all. Wow. Jesus forgave people who didn't ask for it, didn't deserve it, and had completely wronged Him. That is the example we have to follow. If Jesus was able to do it, so should we. C.S. Lewis writes in *The Weight of Glory*, "To be a Christian means to forgive the inexcusable, because God has forgiven the inexcusable in you."[9]

We forgive because we have been forgiven. It is my hope that you have experienced God's forgiveness. If you haven't, now is the time to do it. 1 John 1:9 says, "If we confess our sins, he is faithful and just and will forgive us our sins and purify us from all unrighteousness." If you have never asked God to forgive your sins and you are yet to be part of His

---

[9] Lewis, C.S. *The Weight of Glory.* (New York: Harper Collins, 2001; originally published 1949) p.182

family, don't let this moment pass without asking for God's forgiveness or talking to someone who can help you.

There is one last scenario we need to address: when the person you need to forgive is yourself. You may have carried around the regret of your decisions or actions for years. Maybe your actions were a piece of a larger situation in which you forgave the others involved but have yet to forgive yourself. Maybe it was something that makes you feel dirty and you don't even want to think about it, let alone forgive yourself for it. Maybe it was something that hurt someone you love and you are still bitter toward yourself for the pain you caused. The same truths about forgiving others apply to yourself as well. If you want to experience freedom, you must follow Christ's example of forgiveness – even when it comes to yourself.

Forgiving yourself allows you to move forward and fully accept the grace offered through Jesus. Often deep guilt and shame accompany our sins and because of that, we struggle to forgive ourselves. We judge ourselves and come to the conclusion that we are not worthy of forgiveness. The problem with that mindset is Jesus has already forgiven us. If He was willing to sacrifice His life in order to forgive you, then you need to understand that God's forgiveness is bigger than your guilt and shame. He paid the price on the cross so you don't have to feel guilt or shame anymore. Humble yourself, and let it go.

Think about who you need to forgive. I know it can be extremely painful to even think about that person, but you must in order to begin the process. So think about that person right now and make the decision to forgive them. You don't even need to talk to that person. The decision to forgive is a personal one that doesn't involve that person. It involves you and your heart. So, do it! Make the decision to forgive and remind yourself of that decision as often as you need to.

CHAPTER 8
THE VOID

The Void

Growing up in Southern California, I was blessed to be able to surf at some of the most beautiful beaches and best surfing locations in the world. I was out with some of my buddies a few years ago having a great time surfing and hanging out. The water was crowded because the waves were particularly good that day. Surfers are notorious for not being very good at sharing. Waves are something to be coveted and those who ride them think each wave belongs to him. That day was no different. We all spotted a big wave rolling in, and I quickly decided my desire to ride this nice wave was less of a priority than my safety. With so many people competing for the same wave, it was not worth the risk of getting run into or run over. However, my friend Marco did not share my priorities. He and about five other surfers began paddling for the wave with all their might. Just as the wave was about to break, Marco jumped to his feet and rode down the face of the wave, beating his competitors. He was in for a beautiful ride, but just as he began catching speed another surfer, who did not see him, decided to drop in directly in front of him. The next three seconds seemed to go by in slow motion as Marco collided with the other surfer. With a loud crash they both plunged under the water and after what seemed like minutes they both emerged uninjured. Their boards, however, were a different story. Both boards suffered some pretty severe dings and would definitely need repairs. Both surfers got out of the water, shook hands, and parted ways to deal with their busted boards.

What Marco did next was a little surprising. He went to his truck, slapped some duct tape on the big ding that went all the way through the fiberglass down to the foam, and returned to the water. The duct tape was not enough of a fix for the damage done to his board. In fact, it wasn't a fix at all. In spite of Marco's hopes that the tape would hold, it let water in and destroyed his board even more.

Oftentimes that is exactly what we do. We know there is an issue, but instead of dealing with it and seeking a true fix, we fill our lives with other things. Because we do not see ourselves the right way, we feel inadequate and try to fill that void with people, activities, or other things we feel may help us cope with our perceived lack of value. We do things that make us temporarily feel good, feel valued, or that numb us to our true feelings. We attempt to fill the void so we don't feel empty. But if we are honest, it just leaves us feeling emptier than before. That is because we are not addressing the real issue.

Seeking Approval

One big way we try to fill the void is by seeking approval. We want to be loved, liked, and told we are awesome because we don't feel like we are. We want to hear it from other people and experience it from them. It feels good, and we desire that approval.

Licensed clinical psychologist Jennifer Kromberg wrote in an article for *Psychology Today*, "As humans, once our basic needs are met, much of our conscious and unconscious behaviors are meant to make us feel loved and valued. But this love and value can come from external or internal sources...If enough of your external validation comes from attention, it can become an addiction — a dependence on the affirmations of others in order to feel a sense of worth."[10] What Kromberg means here is that we are wired to seek approval. Even unconsciously, we seek approval and validation from others to confirm our worth. This is a huge one for me.

As a kid, I always wanted to hear what a great job I had done and how wonderful everyone thought I was. Some of my earliest memories are of jumping off the couch as far as I could and timing my jumps when my parents were looking so they would tell me I did a good job. I was gifted athletically, and every time I did something I would ask if I had done alright just to hear them tell me how great I was, even though I knew I had done well. In sports, school, church, skipping rocks, or jumping off the couch, I always sought approval and wanted to hear how great I was. This continued throughout my childhood, into adolescence, and beyond.

I would like to say things have changed now that I am an adult, but they have not. To this day, after each message I preach, I always ask the same question after: "How was my message?" After speaking in the main services at our church on Sundays, I talk with people in the lobby and hear over and over how much they liked the sermon. Then I get home and the first thing I ask my wife is how well I did preaching. I just

---

[10] Kromberg, Jennifer. "Attention Trap Part 1: Narcissism, Validation and Self-Worth." 10 June 2013,
www.psychologytoday.com/ca/comment/887437.

heard from twenty people at church how great I was, but I still ask to get that ego-boosting approval.

I go out of my way to seek approval, and I don't think I am the only one who does this. We try our hardest to get people to like us so we can feel better about ourselves – so our self-image, our worth, and our value will be boosted.

We seek the approval of others on social media. We try as hard as we can to be likable. We spend hours trying to take the right picture, come up with the perfect caption or comment, and do the right things so people will like us. It makes us feel good about ourselves.

One of the major ways we seek approval is through romantic relationships. It feels great to be liked or loved. I remember feeling like I was walking around on a cloud for months after my wife and I first started dating. It feels great to be wanted, and there is immense pressure to do whatever it takes to maintain that approval. That is why many people offer up their bodies so easily. People fill the void in their lives with a significant other or with sexual interactions instead of filling it with the approval that already exists in Christ.

The same goes for the circle of friends we seek to gain approval from. We are willing to compromise our values, consciences, and what we know is right in order to be accepted. We find ourselves doing and saying things we would not normally do or say so people will like us. We so deeply desire love and approval that we don't see ourselves clinging to something that is false. This type of love and approval will let us down and leave us desperate for more.

We seek approval because we want to feel better about ourselves. But our obsession with what people think of us is the quickest way to forget what God thinks of us. When we get caught up in the pursuit of approval from others, we lose sight of the fact that we already have the approval of God through Jesus. In our attempts to win the approval of others, we set aside our Jesus-colored glasses and forget how He sees us. We must learn to do the opposite. Set aside the opinions of others and seek the approval of our King and Savior by putting on Jesus-colored glasses and seeing yourself the way He sees you.

Our Escape

One of the main symptoms of not seeing ourselves correctly is trying to escape from reality and fill the self-worth void in our lives with something other than an actual fix. When any of my daughters get hurt in any way – a bumped head, a fall that scares them, merely witnessing one of their sisters get hurt – they ask for a Band-Aid. We have a healthy stash of all sorts of colorful Band-Aids featuring all their favorite characters for just such occasions. There have been days I have come home and each child has had three different Band-Aids with nothing under them on three different parts of their bodies. Of course these Band-Aids don't fix anything. There is hardly ever actual blood involved at all, but they make great distractions for my daughters. This is pretty normal and completely adorable for three-year-olds, but it is not healthy at all once we grow up. Yet we do this all the time.

We attempt to escape the feelings of inadequacy by escaping from reality. If we can divert our attention and numb our feelings, we can forget about how worthless we feel. This can lead to addiction, pain, and destruction in our lives. Many times, the seemingly glamorous and carefree party lifestyle is really a loud cry stating how much one cares and how empty that person feels. It's a brightly colored Band-Aid over a broken bone.

Dr. Hamid Reza Alavi says in an article in the U.S. National Library of Medicine, "Often, the feeling of people with low self-esteem toward themselves is determined by their current actions. Such people are constantly in need of external positive experiences in order to overcome negative thoughts and feelings they are constantly influenced by."[11] In other words, when we feel worthless we are more likely to turn to other things to fill the void we feel. This is why many rehab facilities begin or end their treatment with self-esteem and substance abuse worksheets. Often they go hand in hand.

Partying and drinking are sedatives to numb insecurities and escape self-doubts. People feel as if their problems disappear during that time. Drugs are another alternative people turn to for a few moments of escape because they allow people to run from the reality of their loneliness and self-doubt.

The problem with this solution is you need more and more of whatever your escape route is or the escape

---

[11] Alavi, Hamid Reza. "The Role of Self-Esteem in Tendency towards Drugs, Theft and Prostitution." The U.S. National Library of Medicine, www.ncbi.nlm.nih.gov/pmc/articles/PMC3905528/.

comes to an end. When the escape stops, you are left to deal with reality or continue spinning downward until hitting rock bottom. Then it doesn't matter how much escape you seek, there is no way out.

This category is not just drugs and alcohol. It can be anything that momentarily gives us the feeling of escape. Maybe your escape from reality doesn't involve drinking or drugs but the creation of a world that doesn't really exist on social media. You can create a euphoric reality that stars someone who isn't you at all to mask your pain in those moments. Or maybe you distract yourself by shopping, eating, playing video games, or even gossiping. It may look totally different but the concept is the same – an escape from the pain of reality.

The Solution

Imagine putting a Band-Aid on a broken bone. If you have a broken bone, you need to see a doctor! The longer you let the Band-Aid distract you, the longer it will take for your bone to heal once you do finally go to the doctor. Filling the void with whatever helps us escape reality just masks and prolongs the problem. The problem is us, and the solution is Jesus. Our feelings of inadequacy, doubt, loneliness, and worthlessness can only be healed by Jesus. When we turn to other sources to fill that void, we do not solve anything. All those distractions fade, and we are left as lonely and broken as before. We need a permanent solution.

We need Jesus in our life, and we must learn to value the approval we have from Him over the approval we get from others. Understanding that God already sees us as amazing and that we do not need to seek approval from the world frees us up to live for Him without focusing on what others think.

Galatians 1:10 says, "Am I now trying to win the approval of human beings, or of God? Or am I trying to please people? If I were still trying to please people, I would not be a servant of Christ."

Trying to win the approval of people is a false pursuit because people change and in the grand scheme of things their opinions don't matter at all. There is only one opinion that matters and here is how He feels about you: "See what great love the Father has lavished on us, that we should be called children of God! And that is what we are! The reason the world does not know us is that it did not know Him."[12] The world is not our standard – God is. And He loves us unconditionally.

That is the only thing that will fix the brokenness in our lives. It doesn't matter how hard we try. We can try distraction after distraction but only one thing can fix it, and that is God. We have a God-shaped void in our lives and the only way to fill it is to fill it with Him. He is the only one who will satisfy us and fill our need for something extra in our lives. We do not feel we are enough, but God says otherwise. He made you in His image and gave you extreme worth and value. He completes you. The only way to allow Him to complete you and fill the void is through Jesus.

---

[12] 1 John 3:1

When feelings of inadequacy overwhelm you and you don't know where to turn, pause and make the decision to turn to Jesus. Decide to see yourself correctly and make decisions based on who you really are. Put on Jesus-colored glasses, and understand that God loves you unconditionally and nothing can fill the void in your life except Him.

Do you find yourself seeking approval from others? Are you wearing any Band-Aids? What are they? Write down the things in your life you might be using to fix your insecurities.

CHAPTER 9
WORRY

Worry

I remember when my wife and I bought our first car. At the time she drove a small, old, beat up pickup truck that had more problems than a soap opera. We worried if we would make it to our destination every single time we sat in it. We worried about how much more money it would cost us. And I worried about the situations my wife might be in if it broke down while she was alone.

We finally decided it was time to upgrade. We went to a dealership to look at some nice used cars and talked to a salesman who was very good at his job. Before we knew it, we were no longer looking at used cars and instead settling on a brand new one, fresh off the lot. I remember joyfully pulling onto the road not worried about the reliability of the vehicle at all, and it felt so nice! But as soon as my mind was cleared from that worry and I was able to think about other things, a big thought popped into my head. How would we afford to make the car payment each month? It hit me hard, and I began hard-core worrying about paying off the car.

Worry can be a vicious monster. Mark Twain summed it up best when he said, "I am an old man and have known a great many troubles, but most of them have never happened."[13] I think we can all relate. There are so many things we can worry about! We worry about family, friends, and enemies. We worry about things we

---

[13] Twain, Mark. Compiled by John P. Holms and Karin Baji. *Bite-Sized Twain Wit and Wisdom from the Literary Legend.* (St. Martin's Press, 1998) p.3

did and regret, and things we didn't do but should have done. We worry about work, health, emotions, and sometimes even how much we worry. And as soon as one worry is cleared up, another one jumps right in and consumes our minds.

We Care Deeply

We tend to worry about the things we care deeply about. When it comes to my kids, I worry big time about their safety, their future, their feelings, and everything that has to do with them because I love them deeply. I also worry about my ministry. Every single detail of my ministry poses yet another worry, and I indulge. Why? Because I care about it deeply.

There are other things I think about but are really not a cause for worry in my life. Take sports for example. There are different types of sports people: those who enjoy playing, talking, and watching sports in general, and those who live and die based on the performance of a specific team. There are teams I cheer for and want to win, but I don't lose any sleep over it when they don't. They don't consume my thoughts or make me worry. I worry about my kids because I love them dearly. But professional sports teams, not so much. Why? Because we only worry about the things we care deeply about.

Insecurity is just another word for worry. We worry about people's opinions of us because we care deeply. We worry about our image, our social media presence, our body type, or who thinks we are attractive. The things we worry about are a direct reflection of how we see ourselves. Our worries reveal what is most important to us. If we saw ourselves the way Jesus sees us, we would not care deeply enough about our image to seek approval from other sources or worry about how others view us.

Change Your Focus

We would cut a huge chunk of worry and anxiety from our lives by simply shifting the things we hold dear. So, how do we change what we deeply care about? We change our focus.

We must believe what Jesus says about us and then truly see ourselves as He sees us. If we care more about what God thinks and says about us than what people think and say about us, insecurities will melt away. That source of concern is removed because it is no longer the focus of what we deeply care about. When we put on Jesus-colored glasses and see ourselves the way He sees us, what we deeply care about shifts. We no longer seek approval in everything we do because we have found it in Christ.

Jesus Himself says not to worry about stuff! But let's be honest, it is difficult because we have been practicing for years. Jesus knew that, which is why he talked specifically about worry in Matthew 6:25-34. Jesus, in preaching the Sermon on the Mount, said the following about worry:

> That is why I tell you not to worry about everyday life—whether you have enough food and drink, or enough clothes to wear. Isn't life more than food, and your body more than clothing? Look at the birds. They don't plant or harvest or store food in

barns, for your heavenly Father feeds them. And aren't you far more valuable to him than they are? Can all your worries add a single moment to your life? And why worry about your clothing? Look at the lilies of the field and how they grow. They don't work or make their clothing, yet Solomon in all his glory was not dressed as beautifully as they are. And if God cares so wonderfully for wildflowers that are here today and thrown into the fire tomorrow, he will certainly care for you. Why do you have so little faith? So don't worry about these things, saying, 'What will we eat? What will we drink? What will we wear?' These things dominate the thoughts of unbelievers, but your heavenly Father already knows all your needs. Seek the Kingdom of God above all else, and live righteously, and he will give you everything you need. So don't worry about tomorrow, for tomorrow will bring its own worries. Today's trouble is enough for today.[14]

In verse 33, He gives the antidote to worry. Instead of worrying, especially about things you cannot control, seek God. Seek God's kingdom, strive to please Him with all you do and in your relationship with Him, and allow God to take care of you. What Jesus says here is to switch your focus. Change what you deeply care about. When Jesus becomes what we deeply care about, He occupies our minds. We begin to think about serving Him and how we can further His mission instead of worrying about all the little things.

---

[14] (NLT)

Worrying can do nothing to help your situation. All worrying does is waste your precious time and energy. Famous Christian Corrie ten Boom, who helped Jews through the Dutch underground during Nazi occupation, said this about worry: "Worry does not empty tomorrow of its sorrow, it empties today of its strength."[15] Worry does nothing to help us, only Jesus can help us and has the power to take care of our situation. Run to him.

Let's change our focus and start seeing ourselves as Jesus sees us. When we put on Jesus-colored glasses, we no longer have any reason to worry. Sure, problems will come up. But when we understand the role God plays in our lives, we are able to rest in Him and set our worries aside. When we say yes to Jesus, we break the chains of worry. When we allow worry to creep in, we momentarily forget who we are. We forget we belong to God and that He cares for us.

Will you still worry? Yes, you are human after all. But that is when you need to put on Jesus-colored glasses to keep from falling into worry and anxiety. Make reminders for yourself and set them around so when you begin to worry, you are quickly reminded of your standing with Christ and His promises. Maybe these reminders are Scriptures, pictures, or an object you can set around your house or in your car. Maybe it's a simple note you can leave yourself or a Bible verse graphic you can put as the background on your phone. I don't know what it is for you, but I would encourage

---

[15] Ten Boom, Corrie. *Clippings from my Notebook: Writings of and Sayings Collected.* (Thomas Nelson, 1982) p.33

you to find something to remind you of God's truth and take you away from a place of worry.

CHAPTER 10
THE RIGHT VIEW

The Right View

Jesus' view of you is the right view. He sees all of you and sees you correctly. We, on the other hand, struggle to see ourselves correctly. He sees us clearly and fully all the time.

Recently, one of the nearby high schools built a new football stadium. It is top-notch and looks more like it belongs to a prestigious university. It has a quality playing surface and track, but the nicest part is the bleachers. There is a great press box, concession stand, open courtyard, ticket booths, and expansive covered seating over about seventy-five percent of the bleachers. The new stadium's grand opening was planned for homecoming night, so it was particularly busy and also happened to be pouring rain. Tons of people were in attendance, and it was a race to get seats. I had volunteered to take tickets for the event, so I asked someone to save a seat for me until I was done. My only request was that my seat be under the covered portion of the stadium. When I was finally able to sit down, I was very thankful to be protected from the rain until I realized something. Large posts holding up the wonderful roof stood every thirty feet or so, and it just so happened that one of these large posts was right in front of me. It totally blocked my view. I saw pieces of the field but was unable to see the whole picture because my view was blocked. Luckily, I had a friend sitting about ten seats over from me, positioned directly between the posts. He could see everything clearly, and when there was a big play he would yell over to me what had happened. He had to relay the full picture to me because I was unable to see it clearly myself.

The same thing happens to us. We are blocked from seeing our true selves. Self-doubts get in our way and we struggle to see the full picture – the real us. But Jesus sees us clearly. He sees the full picture even when we cannot, so He tells us from His vantage point what He sees. We must put on Jesus-colored glasses so we can see ourselves correctly when life gets in the way and our view is blocked.

Freedom Found In The Full Picture

When we feel like everything we do is judged and people look down on us, when we feel worthless and alone, when we feel we are buckling under the pressure to perform, we must remember we are unable to see the full picture. Yes, those feelings are real and painful, but our view of ourselves is blocked. We aren't able to see the full picture of who we are. But Jesus can. He relays what He sees, just as my friend at the football game did for me.

When He looks at you, He sees someone who is amazing. He sees someone who has extreme value, is gifted, and has power to go out in boldness and change the world. He sees someone without a spirit of fear, but of love and power and a strong mind to share the love of Christ with everyone.[16] The Bible says in 1 John 4:16, "And so we know and rely on the love God has for us." Even when we cannot see the full picture

---

[16] 2 Timothy 1:7

of ourselves because of our own sin, God still loves us. Romans 5:8 reminds us of that very clearly when it states, "But God demonstrates his own love for us in this: While we were still sinners, Christ died for us." No matter your situation and circumstance, God still loves you.

Seeing ourselves the right way, the fully-unobstructed way, frees us. It empowers and allows us to understand our worth and our value. The world in which we live will continue to build poles in our line of sight to keep us from seeing ourselves clearly. There will constantly be self-doubts that block you and give you a distorted view of yourself. But Jesus' view is unhindered, and nothing will change the way He sees you.

When you live your life as Jesus sees you and remember to put on Jesus-colored glasses daily, you live with power. You have power over doubt, worry, shame, inadequacies, and everything that prevents you from seeing the real you. You can live with the power and confidence that Jesus sees every time He looks at you. In 2 Timothy 1:7 it says, "For the Spirit God gave us does not make us timid, but gives us power, love and self-discipline." God has given us power to overcome, to not fall victim to situations that arise in our lives.

Looking Past Ourselves To See Jesus

You will be faced daily with the fight to live as Jesus sees you, not as you see yourself. It is a conscious decision to go against our default mode of seeing ourselves poorly. Famous pastor and author Rick

Warren wrote, "God says the only way you're ever going to find yourself is by forgetting yourself and focusing on God. Then you'll not only figure out God; you'll also figure out you."[17] We need to change from thinking about ourselves to thinking about God so we can see ourselves the way He sees us.

We are reminded in Ephesians 2:10, "For we are God's handiwork, created in Christ Jesus to do good works, which God prepared in advance for us to do." We have been saved to do amazing things for God, and He has chosen us. We are also told in Philippians 1:6, "Being confident of this, that he who began a good work in you will carry it on to completion until the day of Christ Jesus." We can have confidence in who we are in Christ!

What if we all lived our lives with confidence in the way Jesus sees us? What if we lived like we really and truly believed what He says about us? Can you imagine the impact we would have on the world? If we were all able to understand what Jesus sees and tap into His view in the way we live our lives, the world would completely change.

Remember to put on Jesus-colored glasses daily and make the choice to see yourself the right way. There will always be obstructions to your vision, but it is a choice to not allow the imperfect picture you see of yourself to tell the story. Gain power from His view of you and go change the world.

---

[17] Warren, Rick. "To Find Yourself, Focus On God." Pastor Rick's Daily Hope Devotional. 28 July 2013. Found on www.pastorrick.com/devotional.

CHAPTER 11
LABELS

Labels

If you have a super organized, Type A personality, you love this device. You dream about it and think it's the best thing in the world. It is a label maker. For those of you who aren't ultra-organized, a label maker prints out a sticker with whatever you type on it so you can label anything. You might find a stapler in an office labeled with a name so well-meaning coworkers won't steal it or cabinets or boxes in a supply closet labeled with the contents. Labels are useful because they can help categorize items and assign parameters to them. They tell you what things are, where they go, what they are able to do, and how to use them.

Just like objects that get labeled, we have labels as well. We are told who we are, what categories we fit into, and what parameters we have. I bet you have dozens of labels, some you've carried for a very long time. Labels are usually given to us by society and by those around us, but we also adopt some on our own. Regardless of where they come from, each of us carries labels that define us and tell us what we are able to do.

Everyone's labels look different and come from different places. But I am sure you can relate to some of these: not athletic, goody-two-shoes, dumb, boring, pretty, weird, mean, smart, not good enough … the list goes on and on. Somewhere along the line, labels were placed on us and have shaped who we are. They impact the way we see ourselves, the way we carry ourselves, and the way we act in light of what we think about ourselves. Too often our labels influence our actions.

As a kid, I gave myself a label that stuck with me for many years. I felt I was not good at reading, which is one of the biggest measuring sticks for a young elementary student. I had zero confidence in my reading ability, so I gave myself the label of "dumb in school." Being homeschooled, I had never actually heard anyone else my age read. I had been comparing myself to my mom. It wasn't until summer camp in the third grade that I heard peers read for the first time and realized I was just like everyone else at my level, in fact better than most. Unfortunately, I had already given myself that label so I carried it around for years, even into high school.

When I got older, coaches told me I wasn't good enough at my sport. I remember my high school baseball coach saying, "You can't hit the broad side of a barn." I took it to heart and wore that label so prominently it ended my hitting career. It was hard to hear, and it hurt deeply. I had spent years training and practicing, and I actually could hit. But I took the label that coach gave me to heart and wore it even though it was false. I internalized that label and made it come true in my life.

That is what happens with labels. We start to believe them no matter how false they may be. Many times the labels we identify as issues in our lives come from childhood or adolescence, but that is definitely not the only time we are labeled. We might identify our childhood labels the quickest because we have carried them the longest, but the truth is we are constantly being handed new labels, even in adulthood. I don't know when you received the labels you carry, but as long as we are around people, we will be labeled.

A few years ago another pastor looked me in the eye and told me I was not cut out for ministry and that maybe it wasn't my calling to be a pastor. He said I wasn't good enough for it and suggested that I get another job in another field. It was devastating. I had spent my life working toward where I was. I had earned a college degree focused on ministry, been ordained, and spoken at camps, chapels, and retreats. In all those years, I had never been told that before. People had affirmed my calling, and I had seen God do amazing things. I felt so strongly that God had called me to ministry and was still calling me to ministry, yet I carried that label around with me for years. It crept up often and made me question myself. In fact, I still find that label popping up at times and begin questioning whether I should really be a pastor, if I really can help people, or if maybe I should just go do something else.

Labels are powerful and have major control over our lives. They lock us in, and they lock us out. They lock us in under their control and make us believe we are destined to live only by our label. In the same way, they lock us out of opportunities because we believe our labels and doubt our ability to live outside them. They determine how we see ourselves and too often are the place from which we derive our value and our identity.

The problem is the place from which we receive our labels. Whether it's from an authority figure, peer, enemy, someone we don't even know, or ourselves, our labels come from people. Not a single person I just listed has the right to label you. People will always hand out labels – that will never change – but they do not have the right to do so.

Who Gets To Label?

The right to label something comes from two places: the creator or the owner. The one who created the object has the right to name it and assign it value. The other rightful labeler is the owner of an object, the one who has purchased something and owns the right to do with it as they please.

I remember very vividly the first *real* baseball mitt I received. I had owned a plastic one before and while I was thankful for it, the new one was the real deal. It was mostly leather, able to catch a hard throw without breaking, and looked super awesome on my hand. When I received the mitt, it already had one label on it placed there by the manufacturer, prominently displaying the brand name. The manufacturer who designed, crafted, and created the mitt placed their name on it so everyone would know it was their creation. I then added a second label to it. By the strong suggestion and wise advice of my parents, I wrote my name and phone number with permanent marker on the outside of one of the fingers so everyone would know who it belonged to. The mitt had two labels – one from the creator, the people who made it, and one from the owner, me.

The same goes for us. The only one with the right to label us is our Creator and our Owner. God is our Creator; He made us and gave us life. He spoke the world into existence and delicately knit you together in your mother's womb. God is your Creator, so He has the right to label you. Next it's your Owner's turn. Jesus paid the ransom for your life by hanging on the cross. He purchased you by paying the ultimate price, and you belong to Him. Therefore, the only One who actually has the right to label you has already done so. Your real label reads *very good*, *amazing*, and *worth it*.

The Only Labels That Matter

You may carry around dozens of labels with you, but how many came from someone who actually had the right to label you? We must peel off the labels given to us by people, society, and ourselves and instead prominently display the labels given to us by our Creator and Owner. It's true that our labels do define us – the problem is when we look at the wrong ones. God has taken His all-powerful label maker and given you the permanent labels of *valuable* and *amazing*, and those are the labels you should be looking at. Too many of us allow the other labels we have been given to crowd out our original labels.

Picture wearing a shirt on which the labels God has already given us are embroidered. Then every time someone hands us a label – *worthless, ugly, failure* – we stick it on our shirts too. Before we know it, we have covered the original labels. We only see those we have been given over the years and believe about ourselves, instead of the truth that came from the One with the right to label us.

Seeing The Right Label

Discovering what God says about us is the first step in taking off the false labels we have been given. When we begin to believe the truth about ourselves, the enemy's lies are debunked and our false labels begin to fall off. We must identify what God says and let go of what others have said that contradicts His truth.

Pastor Ricardo Sanchez summed it up perfectly when he said, "The devil knows your name but calls you by your sin. God knows your sin but calls you by your name."

Take a few moments to think about some of the labels you carry around. Grab a pen and paper and write down labels you carry. To help you think, just examine why you do what you do and question if maybe there is a label behind your actions. Think about how those labels have affected you and how discarding them will impact you in a positive way. Write them down and then write down how you might begin to peel them off and see your God-given labels. Allow your labels to fall off by embracing the permanent labels given to you by your Creator and your Owner – you are amazing.

CHAPTER 12
VIEWING OTHERS

Viewing Others

Sometimes, when we are unable to see ourselves correctly, we are unable to see others correctly either. Not seeing the God-given value of humans or understanding how God sees people is a very dangerous ledge to stand on. That is why Jesus-colored glasses are so important. They are not just for looking at ourselves, but also for looking at the world around us.

If we learn to look through Jesus' lenses when we look at the world, we will catch a fire and passion for those far from Him. Jesus loves, that is who He is. When He looks at you, He loves, and when He looks at the world, He loves. His desire is for everyone to come to Him and experience His love. Once we have grasped that concept, our only logical response is to take His love to the world.

The truth is, every one of us has been assigned a mission. If you call yourself a follower of Christ, then you have a mission. You don't get to argue or decline. It has been assigned, and the only option is to succeed or fail. You can choose not to act on it, but inaction results in failure. Not wanting to complete the mission does not excuse you from the responsibility of its outcome. Just like a spy movie – and I love spy movies – not completing our mission results in deaths, whether we try or simply choose to ignore it altogether.

The awesome part is that fulfilling this mission is the quickest way to satisfaction in our lives because we are doing what we were created to do. God created us on purpose and gave each of us special and unique gifts and talents. We will talk about this more in the next chapter, but we have been given gifts from God that aren't for us. They are to be used to serve God. Fulfillment comes by doing what God created you to do – spreading His good news to all people.

A Father's Love

Each of us should desire to get closer to God. He is our Creator, Father, Protector, Sustainer … and the list goes on and on. There are major benefits to being close with God, and we should all desire a close relationship with Him. But one thing we forget so often is that the quickest way to get close to our Father is to care about His children. Trust me, I am a father.

I love my daughters more than anything in the world. They are so much fun, and every day I look forward to coming home and playing with them. But almost as much fun is watching their interaction and love for their grandparents. If you have kids or if you have grandparents, you know what I am talking about. Grandparents go nuts over their grandkids, and they should. Both my parents and my in-laws absolutely love my kids, and it is awesome.

One night, my father-in-law decided to take us out to dinner at one of my in-laws' favorite restaurants. As soon as we got settled, my kids were immediately entertained by the sugar packets on the table. They stacked them, lined them up, counted them, and were having a great time playing quietly and respectfully with the sugar packets. Not long after, one of the managers came to our table, took all the sugar packets from the kids, and scolded them as he did. We were all surprised because the kids were not being crazy or disrespectful at all. As he walked away, he made a backhanded comment about how my children were acting. At that very moment, my father-in-law decided it was time to leave. My kids' Papa loves them more than anything, and he wasn't going to handle someone insulting them. He respectfully informed the manager that if his granddaughters were not welcome, then he wasn't welcome either. So, we all got up and headed to another restaurant down the street. Without telling anyone at the new restaurant what had happened, they greeted my kids, gave them little toys to keep them entertained, and even let them peek over the counter to watch the cook in action. The girls had a blast, and dinner turned out to be a great experience.

Which restaurant do you think we are most likely to go back to? Of course the second one! Why? Because the quickest way to a father is to care about his children. If we want to get close to God, we must care about His children. We cannot pretend people do not exist, are not important, or don't have value if we expect to get close to their Father.

We have this weird idea that people who seclude themselves are somehow more advanced and holy. It's as if we think people who spend all their time in church are the most righteous, or a monk who spends all his time secluded in the mountains is more spiritual. But that is not true at all. Seclusion was never the goal. Serving people is the job God has called us to. We exist to point people to Jesus, and that can't be done from a mountaintop. We are called to put on Jesus-colored glasses when we look at the world and see people for who they are – deeply loved by God and worth His sacrifice on the cross.

We all know this world is a rough place to live and that heaven is perfect. So why doesn't God just take us straight there when we accept Him? Pastor and author Rick Warren answers that question by reminding us that there are only two things you can do here on earth that you cannot do in heaven; the first thing is sin, and the second is tell people about Jesus. Warren then asks, "Why do you think you are here? It's definitely not to sin; so what is it?"

We exist to love and share Christ with the people around us. This means we must intentionally put ourselves in places where we can be with people who do not know Christ. Now, does this mean we have an excuse to be at wild parties, clubs, and places we know we will end up doing things we shouldn't? No, of course not. Each of you knows what you can handle. Don't go someplace where you will be dragged down, but do get out of your bubble and interact with people who need Jesus.

I intentionally go to the gym in town where most people go. Being a coach at the high school, I have private access to the gym at school for free. I also have friends with equipment in their garages and could work out with them for free as well. But I intentionally purchased a gym membership in town because I know I will meet people who are far from Christ. Whether I am on the treadmill next to someone, working out with someone on the bench press (inevitably lifting a significantly smaller amount of weight than them), or putting my stuff in the locker next to someone, I am interacting with people. And many of them do not have a relationship with God. Does that change how I treat them? No! God has called us to love people whether they think like us, act like us, or not.

If you seclude yourself from the world, you can't fulfill your God-given mission. God has called us to love. If we are not sharing the good news of Christ, we cannot say we are loving people, and we can't expect to get closer to their Dad either. When we see people the way Jesus sees them, our only true response can be to love them enough to share Jesus with them.

It's Not New

Many churches do not see the world this way and it is, in some ways, a bit of a radical concept to them. But this is not a new idea by any stretch of the imagination, and I didn't invent it. The idea of going out and being with people and loving people has been around for a very long time. It came from Jesus, and He is the one who shows us how to do it.

If you read the Gospels (Matthew, Mark, Luke, and John) in the Bible, you see that Jesus did not spend most of His time in the temple. He spent His time with people – loving them, healing them, and teaching them. He went around breaking down stereotypes of what it meant to love both God and people. Many of the church people of the day were exactly like church people of today. They did not want to be seen with or associate with sinners. They judged people and steered clear of them. But that is definitely not how Jesus acted.

In Matthew 9:9-13 we see this very clearly:

> As Jesus was walking along, he saw a man named Matthew sitting at his tax collector's booth. "Follow me and be my disciple," Jesus said to him. So Matthew got up and followed him. Later, Matthew invited Jesus and his disciples to his home as dinner guests, along with many tax collectors and other disreputable sinners. But when the Pharisees saw this, they asked his disciples, "Why does your teacher eat with such scum?" When Jesus heard this, he said, "Healthy people don't need a doctor—sick people do." Then he added, "Now go and learn the meaning of this Scripture: 'I want you to show mercy, not offer sacrifices.' For I have come to call not those who think they are righteous, but those who know they are sinners."[18]

We have to understand that during this time, a tax collector was someone seen as a thief and a horrible person. They almost had their own category when it came to how bad they were in the eyes of the Jewish people. There were sinners, and then there were tax collectors. Jesus interacted with some people who were not considered "right" as He walked around town, but it didn't stop there. Jesus went even further and attended a party at Matthew's house. He hung out with the people who, for many Christians, would not be allowed in church or be acceptable to hang out with at all. And the church people of His day were appalled.

---

[18] (NLT)

They questioned Jesus for spending time with and loving people who were not like them. But Jesus completely shut them down and taught us how we are supposed to think and act when it comes to non-believers. Jesus came for people who do not know Him, and that is our mission as well. People who think they have it all together are so self-righteous they don't see a need for Jesus. So why is He even there? If they don't need Him, why did He come? Well, Jesus said He came to seek and save those who are lost. If someone does not even acknowledge that they are lost, they are not in a place where they can be found and saved. Too often we, as Christians, find ourselves hanging out with and associating only with other church people, some who look much like the Pharisees we read about. Did Jesus die for everyone? Yes, of course He did. But as He demonstrates with Matthew the tax collector, His mission was for the sinners and disreputable people. He came for people who knew they weren't close to God and were known as sinners in need of a savior. Every single one of us needs to learn from and be reminded of this amazing example. We must begin seeing the world the way He sees the world – as a rescue mission.

So many people are lost, and we live in a world that is hopeless. All you have to do is turn on the evening news to see that people are running out of hope. People need something to save them, and most people will admit things are not right. It is our job to simply introduce them to Jesus.

A Need To Be Found

When I was about eight years old, I remember a very scary moment for our family. I had just finished a baseball game at a local elementary school. It was a large area, and there were a lot of people there for various activities. When the game ended, I went home with my dad, and my mom went to run some errands. When we were almost home, my dad suddenly remembered that something was missing – my little sister. There had been a miscommunication between my parents as to who was taking my five-year-old sister with them, and we realized we did not know where she was. This was before everyone had cell phones, so we couldn't just call my mom and confirm if my sister was with her. So my dad immediately turned around and sped back to the field. He pushed his 1969 Camaro to do what it was capable of. Taking stop signs as suggestions and red lights as yellows, we made it back to the field quickly and ran down from the parking lot in search of my sister. We immediately spotted her. She was off by herself just walking and kind of playing in the dirt with her feet as she went. My dad ran over to her and stopped about ten feet away. As soon as she noticed him, she burst into tears and ran into his open arms.

She was lost and scared, and she knew it. She knew something was very wrong. She didn't need anyone to tell her she was lost. She didn't need anyone to yell at her with a megaphone, hold a giant sign, or scold her for being lost. All she needed was to be found. She simply needed to be reunited with her father and be wrapped up in his arms.

We live in a world where people are lost. They don't need to be yelled at and told how lost they are; they simply need to be found. Our job is to love people and point them toward Jesus, where they can be wrapped up in His loving arms and find the same saving grace we have found. They, too, can be shown what it is like to wear Jesus-colored glasses and see themselves the way Jesus sees them.

When we truly understand what we look like to Jesus, we can see the world through those same lenses and discover the love He has for others. We must fight complacency, go beyond our walls, and live in light of our Jesus-colored glasses.

So, think about where you can go to be around people who do not know God. Think about how you can show them the love of Christ and how you can be involved in guiding them into His loving arms.

CHAPTER 13
CONQUERORS

Conquerors

God doesn't want you to just exist and feel good about yourself. He has gifted you for a reason. He wants you to use your talents to make a major impact for Him.

The Bible says in Romans 8:37 that in Christ, despite all the trials we face, we are more than conquerors. When life throws overwhelming situations at us, when we are torn down from every angle and we feel small, we need to remember that we are conquerors. No matter what life throws at us, we do not have to merely survive. We can thrive.

That is my prayer for you. I hope that in understanding your worth and value, you don't just reach the point where everything is OK and you feel fine about yourself but that you would realize you are amazing and have amazing potential that needs to be unlocked and let out. It's not that you are just OK; it's that you are a conqueror!

You may understand that He loves you and that your identity is in Him but still wonder why He wants to use *you*. God is overjoyed to use you because you have unique gifts and talents that are different from anyone else. You are a one-of-a-kind diamond, waiting to shine and show people your Creator. The belonging you receive from being part of God's family should empower you to take the world by storm for Him. The fact is, what you alone have to offer is invaluable. God made you unique and special and has given you gifts unique to you. God has shaped you exactly how He wants you.

Shaped For A Purpose

Some of my most prized possessions are my surfboards. I have five surfboards and am often asked by non-surfers why I have so many. Here is why: Each board is completely different and unique. They are different lengths, have different numbers of fins, and have different shapes. They were all custom shaped for a specific purpose. Each board performs differently and was made for different types of waves and conditions. I have so many types of boards because I use them in different ways. The same thing goes for each one of us.

Each of us, just like my boards, was shaped differently on purpose for a purpose. We are all made uniquely different for the purpose of serving God, and serving God looks different for each of us based on our shape.

Now, it is fully possible for you to understand the beauty of your uniqueness and the need to use your gifts but have no clue what your shape is. That is OK. I want to help you discover how God has shaped and gifted you. There are five simple questions you can ask to begin discovering how God has gifted you.

What do I like doing?

It is simple, what do you enjoy doing? God is not going to gift you with something you hate and have no interest in. That wouldn't be much of a gift at all. As a kid, I saw people in church who just looked angry all the time, as if they never had any fun and didn't want anyone else to have fun either. So naturally I thought in order to surrender to God and serve Him, I had to give up all fun. But that is just not true. God wants you to enjoy what you do.

It says in John 10:10 that the enemy wants to steal from you, kill you, and destroy you but that Jesus wants you to experience life to the fullest. He wants you to be fulfilled. So what is it you enjoy doing? When I first entered youth ministry as a student, I discovered not all church people were angry and hated fun. I knew I had found my people and my place. Here I am, years later, and I still love youth ministry. I love what I do.

Take a quick mental inventory or write down some things you enjoy doing. It shouldn't be that difficult to come up with what you enjoy.

Next you have to ask yourself, *What am I good at?*

Some of you might immediately react by saying, "Nothing. I really can't think of anything I am good at." But when you say that you are severely undermining God. God literally spent time crafting you exactly how He wanted you. There is no way He just forgot to give you something to be good at. Every single one of us is good at something.

For you it may be music. For me not so much – I can't even clap on beat. When I start singing, people usually leave. Maybe you are good at athletics or academics or talking. I don't know what it is, but you are good at something.

I know because the Bible says in 1 Peter 4:10-11, "Each of you should use whatever gift you have received to serve others, as faithful stewards of God's grace in its various forms. If anyone speaks, they should do so as one who speaks the very words of God. If anyone serves, they should do so with the strength God provides, so that in all things God may be praised through Jesus Christ. To Him be the glory and the power forever and ever."

Keep in mind that what you enjoy and what you are good at must go hand-in-hand as you discover what gifts God has given you. Like I said, I am terrible at music so just because I love to sing doesn't mean anyone else will enjoy my singing. On your way to finding your gifting, both factors should work together.

So take the list of things you enjoy doing and put a checkmark next to the ones you are good at or are able to get good at with practice and work.

Next, as you look around at the world, ask yourself this: *What frustrates me about the world?*

When you look around, what makes you think, "That's not right"? What bothers you deeply? What do you really feel something must be done about? I am not talking about people not using their blinker or the fact that it's socially unacceptable to wear pajamas all day. This should be something that truly gets your blood flowing and makes you really want to do something about it.

For me, it was the youth in the church being overlooked. I had seen it too many times. Students were seen as just a commodity used to serve the rest of the church. They were viewed as the church of tomorrow – as if their worth and value hadn't materialized yet because they were not fully grown up. I couldn't sit by and watch. I needed to do something about it so I became a youth pastor.

We are all bothered by something that is not right, but being bothered isn't enough. Too often, we see something unjust or that needs to be done and just tell someone else as if it's their job to do something about it. That is not how it works. When something bothers us and stirs us up inside, we need to step up and do something about it. It is part of figuring out our shape.

What is it that stirs you up inside? Think about the things you see around you. What do you see that needs to be fixed? Again, not pet peeves or annoyances, but real issues that need solving. Write a few of those down or make a mental note as you get closer to figuring out your shape and gifting.

Follow that question up by asking this: *What is in front of me right now?*

What opportunities are in front of you? Too often, we look to the future to figure out how we can serve God when there are real opportunities right now. We tend to come up with nice plans for the future and set benchmarks we must hit before our plan can become a reality. We tell ourselves when we have money, then we can do something. When we graduate, get a new car, or have kids ... then we can serve God with our talents. We spend all this time making perfect little plans when all God is asking for is our hands. God doesn't want to hear about your plans to serve Him someday. He wants you to actually serve Him.

I have a friend who is a very organized and tidy person. She keeps things neat and actually enjoys doing it. A few years ago she was at her church and ran across something she couldn't overlook. She opened a door to a large resource room that was very well stocked but incredibly unorganized. The room was a total mess, and no one could find what they needed. Her first reaction was shock because the mess bothered her deeply, and her second reaction was to do something about it. She ended up organizing and developing a system for that room and has now expanded it, trained others on it, and is in charge of running the resource room at her church.

There are many opportunities all around you, and sometimes all you need to do to see them is to change your focus. Have you ever held something too close to your face and not been able to see it because your eyes can't focus and instead end up looking right past it? The same goes for the opportunities around us. Sometimes we need to change our focus to be intentional about seeing them.

When you take the opportunities around you, you might discover something you like and are good at. Maybe you have never thought about it before, but trying new things and taking opportunities can open you up to whole new worlds of possibility and interest. So, think about what opportunities are around you to begin serving God. Think outside the box, make a list, and develop a plan for getting involved.

The last question you need to ask yourself is simple. *Who am I doing it for?*

Who are you going to live for? Is it God, or is it you? Too often I find myself doing things for the benefit of me. But that is the opposite of what the Bible tells us. We must seek to serve God instead of serving ourselves.

When I was in high school, the room we met in was multipurpose, and we had to stack our chairs after the service every Sunday. I absolutely hated stacking chairs! But week after week I would help out and make sure everyone saw me doing it. If someone carried two chairs, I carried three. And I wasn't very subtle about it. The whole time I stacked chairs I was just hoping people would notice how awesome I was and what a servant's heart I had. I hated the task, but I loved the opportunity to boost my image. I wanted others to think I was awesome, and I used the act of "service" to achieve that.

As followers of Christ, it is less about what we say and more about what we do. In Luke 6, the Bible talks about the fruit a healthy tree produces versus the fruit a bad tree produces. We can say we follow Christ and our decisions revolve around Him, but the fruit in our lives tells the true story. You cannot fake it to God because who you choose to live for, whether it's yourself or something other than God, will be plainly seen. We must make sure we choose to do something that glorifies God.

You may be good at something that glorifies something other than God. Maybe it glorifies a sin or something

God created, rather than God Himself. That is a great gauge for realizing maybe that is not what God has gifted you to do. Maybe there is another application of that skill that would change the object of its glorification, so it is important to ask the question.

Discovering Your Shape

So, if you are trying to figure out your shape, ask yourself: What do I like doing? What am I good at? What frustrates me about the world? What is in front of me right now? And who am I doing it for? That is a quick and simple guide to figuring out how God has shaped you.

Also, you need to try different things. You will probably not just wake up with a revelation from God about what you should be doing. Of course He can do that, but that is not how He usually works. We also need to seek God in all of this. Ask Him to reveal your gifts and what you are supposed to do to make an impact for Him. He will reveal how you can serve Him.

You are more than a conqueror in Christ, and He wants you to live like it. Go out and find the power that comes from Him. You belong to Him and have nothing to fear. You were not created to just exist; you were created to thrive and be an amazing witness for Christ. Do not settle for being merely OK with yourself and where you are. Be a conqueror and do big things for God.

CHAPTER 14
GETTING REAL

Getting Real

Once you understand your extreme worth and value, it is so important to put yourself in an environment that will foster that understanding. We cannot do life alone, which means we must find people to help us on our journey of seeing ourselves the way Jesus sees us.

One of the biggest obstacles to seeing yourself correctly is a lack of authenticity. When you are unable to be real with yourself and admit who you really are, you end up lying to yourself and struggling to see yourself the right way. You must be able to be authentic with yourself.

Another way we struggle with authenticity is with other people. We do not want to let people see the real us so we become someone we are not and perpetuate our lack of self-image. We must be authentic with other people and surround ourselves with people who are willing to do the same.

The other huge way we lack authenticity is with God. When we are unable to be real with ourselves and with others, too often we are not real with God either. We do not admit our need for Him or trust Him to be our firm foundation. That is why authenticity is a major key to seeing ourselves correctly and growing in our relationship with Christ.

It is essential to find a place where you can be real. If we continually lie to ourselves, others, and God, we will never see the true us. Authenticity is crucial in keeping a correct view of ourselves and seeing the world correctly, so it needs to become a reflex for us. That is why you need to find a church to plug into and get involved. It is vital that you find a church community where you can be real and your worth and value is reinforced.

Real With Self

Most of us are conditioned to be fake from a very young age, especially if we grew up in church. It is ingrained in us. One of the biggest areas we fake it is to ourselves. We lie to ourselves the most. We struggle to see ourselves the way Jesus sees us and in so doing, we lie to ourselves about our value, our worth, our potential, and our standing with God and others.

Ph.D. Cortney S. Warren writes in an article for *Psychology Today*, "Humans are masters of self-deception. We fool ourselves into believing things that are false—and—we refuse to believe things that are true. In fact, we lie to ourselves about everything… And, most of the time, we are completely unaware of the rampant lying going on in our own minds."[19]

Not being real with ourselves can drive us into depression, anxiety, and bad choices. Going through one of the toughest times in my life, when my self-worth was next to nothing, I still knew all the right things in my head. I had been trained to see truth. I knew truth, and I even taught truth to others as I would

---

[19] Warren, Courtney S. "How Do I Know When I Am Lying To Myself?" 28 May 2014. https://www.psychologytoday.com/us/blog/naked-truth/201405/how-do-i-know-when-i-am-lying-myself.

speak in churches, chapels, and camps. But I wasn't able to be real with myself about my own issues and about how Jesus saw me. I knew the truth in my head, but it had not made its way to my heart. I only went deeper and deeper into self-doubt and depression until God allowed my circumstances to change, and then I was able to see what God was trying to teach me. When I was finally able to be real with myself, my self-image began to turn around, and I was able to see clearly again.

We must seek truth. Jesus said the truth sets you free[20]. We are slaves to the lies we tell ourselves. The truth is the only thing that will free us – truth about ourselves, truth about God, truth about His Word, and truth about this world. We must soak in and live by God's truth, which means we need to read it, study it, and hear it spoken often.

You must find a place where you are able to be real with yourself by learning God's truth. Find a community where the Word of God is preached and you are able to listen and soak it in. God's Word is the ultimate truth and in order to be real with ourselves, we must know that truth and be in a community of believers that focuses on it. Do not compromise on truth. If a church wants to bend the truth, that is between them and God, but it is not a healthy environment for you and will not foster honesty with yourself.

---

[20] John 8:32

Real With Others

I learned many things from growing up in the church, and many of those things prepared me for my ministry today. Unfortunately, one of the biggest things I learned growing up in the church was how to fake it. I guarantee you know exactly what I am talking about if you grew up in church.

I remember many Sundays heading to church when things were a mess. Now, if you have ever been to church, you know it is always a rush getting there on time. No matter how early we planned to leave, my family was definitely always in a rush. Things didn't go well at the house before we left. My sister and I couldn't find anything to wear, my mom ran around frantically trying to get everyone ready, and my dad worked on something completely unrelated to getting us out the door on time. Tensions were high. My dad was mad at my mom for not having his shirt ironed, and mom was mad at my dad for not ironing his own shirt or bothering to help us all get out the door. My sister was mad because she didn't want to wake up, and I tried to find the most creative ways to annoy and provoke everyone, making the situation worse. We finally got in the car and World War III commenced all the way to church. My sister and I fought, and my parents fought and scolded us kids for fighting all at the same time. Right before we got out of the car, my dad would turn around and look at us in the back seat with his I'm-not-messing-around look and say, "We will pull ourselves together, and we will go into church happy."

As we walked into church recovering from the battle that just took place, we were greeted with the same question every church attendee across the country is asked: "How are you guys doing this morning?"

With the biggest smiles all of us could put on we replied, "We are doing *great*, everyone is fine, and it is a great day to worship God." They said something like, "That is great to hear, I am doing amazing as well," and we went on our way.

I bet you can relate. Churches are notoriously bad at fostering authenticity among members. Unfortunately, if we have issues seeing ourselves clearly, we *need* people around us to lean on. We need people to build us up and help us see who God created us to be. If we can't be vulnerable with others about our struggles, then how will our struggles ever be fixed? We also need to surround ourselves with people who will be real with us as well. Authenticity is a two-way street. We must place ourselves in a community that is intentional about authenticity and understands the importance of being real.

We should all strive to be real, especially if we struggle with self-image (which, if we are real, most of us do). We need real, authentic relationships with people who will build us up and help us see ourselves correctly. When we are in a real environment, we receive encouragement from those around us, and we all need encouragement. We are able to share the burden with others. You don't have to do life alone, and you shouldn't. Those who are there for you will remind you of your worth when things get in the way and truth is clouded. Also, when we are involved in a culture of realness and experience other people's transparency, we receive encouragement from the fact that we are not alone. We hear other people's struggles and realize we are in this difficult thing called life together; we are not weird for feeling the way we do because others do as well!

Being real is not easy and it can be uncomfortable, especially if it's a new concept for you. So, how do you be real with others? Being real means sharing and talking about what is really going on in your real life. Be transparent and authentic about your successes and your struggles. Some things you might push yourself to be honest about are your habitual sins. You know, the ones you just keep going back to no matter how hard you try to stop. These are usually the hardest to be real about because they are probably ongoing, and no one wants to admit the sins they are currently involved in. But that is just one more reason why you need to be real about them. We must learn to be candid about some of the specific self-doubts we have as well. Tell people how you truly feel on the inside. Being real also means being honest about your past and the struggles you have faced. You are probably cringing right now, and I understand, because it is extremely difficult to deal with and talk about! But that is part of being real – talking about our past, present, and future.

So, how do you find someone you can be real with? The first step in finding authentic relationships and community is by going first. Lead the way in authenticity by being authentic. It can be uncomfortable to share our soft spots with others, but, like everything, it gets easier with practice. Being real is so worth it. Every time I have been vulnerably real with someone, a door has opened to a whole new level of friendship and community that wasn't there before. Those whom I have shared my vulnerability with have responded with vulnerability and realness themselves. Everyone has the potential to be real, but many people need to be shown how. I am not saying you should bare your soul to the next person you meet – it requires trust and friendship to begin with. Not everyone will make the choice to be real, even if you are. You must use discernment. Make sure the person you are confiding in is someone who will love you and not condemn you. It may take time to decide if a person is someone you can trust before you share your deepest issues with them.

It is important to keep that in mind as well when we are the person someone else is confiding in. We are all sinners in need of a savior and have all been messed up by sin. It is our job to point others to Jesus, not to act like we *are* Jesus. We do not have the right to condemn. As fellow sinners, we only have the right to be real and show compassion. Be someone worthy of hearing someone's deepest thoughts, secret actions, and insecurities. Don't gossip about others – it doesn't breed trust. When you gossip to someone, it says you can't be trusted not to turn around gossip about them. Being real is difficult. If someone has trusted you, be worthy of that trust.

Get real with someone and lean on them to get you through tough times, to receive encouragement, and to be reminded of who you are. This requires finding a church where that can happen. I used to have a stereotype of church in my mind as a place where I had to look and act a certain way in order to be respected. It wasn't until college that I found a church where being real was encouraged, and I learned how church is supposed to be. Since then I have modeled my ministries after that exact vision. I believe realness is essential for connecting with God and experiencing all He has for us. We must be real, and we must find a church where being real is encouraged and normal.

Real With God

We often fake it with God as well. This is crazy because He literally knows everything. But we still do it. We fake it to Him and struggle being real with Him. We think because we are messed up and have done (or are doing) things God would not be happy with, we are unworthy of His love. We feel like we have to clean ourselves up before we can come to God, when in reality we just need to come to God.

God loves us unconditionally, and while we do have a sin problem, He is the only cure for that problem. We need to be real with God because He created us, loves us, and sent His son to die for us. God is not out to get us and judge us all the time. No one measures up, and He knows that. That is exactly why He is not out to get us but rather desires to save us. We need to be real with God by trusting Him, believing what He says about us, and living accordingly. That is not to say God doesn't want us to live righteously or that He doesn't see sin as bad, because He does and it is. But the Bible says God doesn't want to see any of us die, but instead wants to see all of us come to repentance through Jesus[21]. It is a daily choice we must make, to be real about our need for a savior and turn to Jesus. That is what it means to be real with God.

---

[21] 2 Peter 3:9

Find a place where you can be real. Find a church where you can be real with yourself, with God, and with others. The environments you put yourself in can either help your self-image or harm it. Choose an environment where your worth and value are fostered, cared for, and groomed. We need to be in community – and not just any community, but one where we can be authentically led to Christ. If you are not currently attending a church, find one. If you are currently attending a church but feel as if you cannot be real, find a new one. If you are in a church where you can be real but you are not, change the way you act in church. Get involved and be authentic.

CHAPTER 15
THE RIGHT VIEW EVERY DAY

The Right View Every Day

Here is where it gets difficult. How do we put on Jesus-colored glasses daily?

When I was a kid, my parents took my sister and me to get our eyes checked. It was the first time we had been to the eye doctor, and we were both a bit nervous. I had always had pretty good vision and was confident the doctor would confirm that. My sister, on the other hand, had complained from time to time that things were a little bit blurry. When the doctor checked us, my assessment was exactly as I had predicted. However, my sister's vision was a shock to us. She had such poor vision in one eye that she is considered legally blind in that eye. It was crazy that she lived with it for so long and had become so used to it that not seeing clearly was normal for her. When she put glasses on, she was amazed at the detail the world around her held. It was life changing for her.

Unfortunately, she sometimes still forgot to put in her contacts or wear her glasses. She was so accustomed to not wearing them that she didn't, and she frequently had to be reminded to put them on.

The same thing applies to us. Once you have been introduced to Jesus-colored glasses and have seen yourself clearly, your life is changed. But just like how my sister forgot to put on her glasses, we also forget to put on our Jesus-colored glasses. We are so accustomed to not seeing ourselves correctly, it becomes normal and we forget that there is another way. We must break that habit and find ways to be reminded daily to wear Jesus-colored glasses, even when we don't want to.

New Habits

Obviously, we could just remind my sister to put her glasses on by setting an alarm or leaving a note on the mirror. I wish it were as simple as setting an alarm to remind ourselves to put on Jesus-colored glasses, but it's not. So, how do we remind ourselves?

First, we must change our muscle memory. In sports, when you do something over and over so many times your muscles remember what to do without you consciously telling them, we call that muscle memory. The problem comes when we do something incorrectly and our mechanics need to change to get better results. It is hard to just change it. Instead, we need to create a new pattern and get our muscles to remember a new way. We need to change our muscle memory. The same goes for the conditioning of our brain when it comes to how we see ourselves. We must change our muscle memory from running toward a place of self-doubt to running toward Jesus. Instead of falling deeper and deeper into our poor view of ourselves, we must condition ourselves to run to Jesus. Like any other habit, you must do it over and over again until it becomes natural. When you feel yourself slipping into old patterns, make the decision to see yourself the way Jesus sees you. This may mean calling a friend who can remind you of your worth or reading God's Word. We can be reminded to put on Jesus-colored glasses by simply changing who or what we run to when those feelings of inadequacy arise. Continue to run to Jesus and make that the new norm in your life.

Second, we can be reminded to put on Jesus-colored glasses by getting into God's Word – opening the Bible and reading what He has to say about us and about the world. There is no greater reminder than hearing from God Himself. Too often, Christians will cry out to God for an answer when He has left an answer book they never open. Get in the habit of reading God's Word daily and soaking in His truths. Set aside a time to sit down and read His Word because if you don't set that time aside, it won't happen. We get so busy that reading God's Word oftentimes becomes a last priority. I am very guilty of this myself. Sometimes, I will have the best intentions of reading the Bible and then out of the blue I'll stop and later realize it has been weeks since I've read. You can download a Bible app to your phone and have it send you reminders so you can read it right then and there, straight from your phone. You can even have it read to you and all you have to do is listen. Make it a priority, because reading and hearing God's Word is an excellent reminder to put on Jesus-colored glasses.

Next, surround yourself with people who will remind you. We can put reminders all around us but the best reminder to do anything comes from others. I am notorious for not getting things done around the house. I will see something in the yard that needs to be fixed, cleaned, or whatever, and I will put it on my to-do list. I will plan to do it, put it on the calendar, and even add reminders to my phone, but for some reason I still put it off and don't do it until my wife reminds me. When she lovingly looks me in the eye and says, "Hun, I think it's time you go out and fix that," I am reminded of its seriousness and necessity and it finally gets done. When we have people in our lives who remind us to put on Jesus-colored glasses, it makes it a lot easier to remember. We need to surround ourselves with people who will care about us and remind us of who we are in Christ. Join a small group, get involved with a ministry team, do something to surround yourself with people who will be wonderful reminders to put on Jesus-colored glasses.

What Do We Do When They Get Knocked Off?

It is so easy to forget to put on our Jesus-colored glasses and so easy to slip into the habit of not seeing ourselves correctly. That is why it is critically important that we are intentional about reminding ourselves and putting them on daily. But what happens when we don't just accidentally forget to put them on, but they actually get knocked off?

It will inevitably happen. No matter how hard you try to wear Jesus-colored glasses and see yourself the way He sees you, at one time or another, they will get knocked off.

When I was in college, I had the privilege of working with Fellowship of Christian Athletes as a coach for one of their sports camps. The camp was hosted at UCLA and was a great week of meeting athletes from all sports and personally pouring into middle- and high-school-aged baseball players. One of the players we had at the baseball portion of the camp was named George. He left an impression on me that I will never forget.

George was an extremely intelligent young man with a huge heart, was liked by everyone, and loved God. He was one of those people you want to be around because he loved everyone and was a genuinely nice person. However, George wasn't like the other players. He had cerebral palsy, so walking and moving were very difficult for him. Due to his physical condition, he had never played baseball before. He chose it because it looked fun to him, and he was willing to give it his best shot. George was absolutely incredible. He worked harder than anyone and was determined to catch, throw, and hit the ball. During one of the practices, George wanted to get up to the plate and hit the ball in a game setting like everyone else. So, we put him up to bat and had the pitcher scoot in and give him a nice, soft pitch. George missed the first couple pitches but finally connected and hit a ground ball to the third baseman. He yelled with excitement as he ran toward first base. But he didn't make it very far before he fell flat on his face.

Everyone paused for a moment as they looked on, wondering if they should do something, but what they saw next was amazing. George quickly struggled to stand back up and continue running. He took a few more steps before falling flat again. The third baseman fielded the ball but immediately dropped it, picked it up, and dropped it again, all the while watching George run and trying to stall for time. Everyone in attendance knew what was happening, and it was beautiful. George gave all the effort he had to get back up, run a few steps, fall, and do it again. As he was almost to first base, the third baseman lobbed the ball high over the first baseman's head and out of bounds so George could reach base safely. George finally reached first base after falling many times and struggling to run, all the while giving every bit of effort he possessed.

As he stepped on the base he threw his hands in the air in victory. The entire baseball portion of the camp stormed the field and rallied around George. As the tough college baseball player in his early twenties who was coaching this camp, my only response was to let the tears stream down my face as I watched one of the most beautiful scenes I had ever witnessed and learned one of the most important lessons of all time from an incredible human.

You will fall, you will fail, you will have your Jesus-colored glasses knocked off. Life is hard, and there will be days when you struggle to see yourself clearly. There will even be days when the struggle is compounded by something being done or said that knocks you down and tears you up. But as George taught me, when you get knocked down, no matter how tough the circumstances are against you, you need to get back up. We are only defeated when we choose to stay down.

One of my favorite movies is *Batman Begins*, and one of my favorite quotes comes from Bruce Wayne's father. As he picks up young Bruce after a bad fall, he says, "Why do we fall, Bruce? So we can learn to pick ourselves back up again." It is something we must learn because we will fall, and many times the fall is simply an opportunity to learn to pick ourselves back up. Sure, it hurts. When your glasses get knocked off, there is usually some pain involved caused by whatever was done. But guess what? Jesus wins. We know the end of the story, and we are on the winning team. We have victory in Jesus, and we need to get back up and live in His victory daily.

Getting Back Up

So, how do you get back up? Constantly and confidently. Constantly, because the world we live in is not easy and our self-image is something we will always deal with. We will be knocked down often and we must get back up just as often as we are knocked down. It must be a constant theme in our lives. We are constantly going to have to get back up, just as George did multiple times on that ninety-foot run, and we must do it just as he did, with confidence. When you get back up and wear your Jesus-colored glasses again, do it with confidence. We have confidence in Jesus because He has beaten sin, beaten death, and is sitting on the throne next to God the Father. In Him we have confidence that whatever the world throws at us we will overcome. When the enemy knocks you down, get back up. Constantly and confidently. You are a child of the King.

We all have a past. Some pasts are worse than others. I have no idea what your past looks like, but what I do know is this: Your past does not have to affect your future. You may feel that because of what was done to you or you have done in the past, God cannot use you in the future. But that is an outright lie the enemy wants you to believe. You are incredible, you are amazing, you are not an accident, and God wants to use you to reach people for Him.

I once heard of a guy who had a really ugly past. You may think yours is bad, but this guy's was worse. This man was angry and wanted to show the world how angry he was to the point where he killed people and rallied others to murder as well. You could say he was like the leader of a gang that did incredibly violent acts and wasn't shy about letting people see those acts. But one day this man had an encounter with God, and his life was never the same. His past was about as messed up as anyone's could be, but from that day forward he dedicated himself to serving God.

I have to confess, this man I am talking about is very well known. His name is Paul, and he wrote most of the New Testament. It is an incredible story. Paul went on to do some absolutely incredible things. His past was as dark as they come, but his future was brighter than anyone could imagine, and God wants to give you a bright future as well. It doesn't matter how bad your past is, today is a new day and the life ahead of you is an opportunity to live for Christ and be used by Him. God wants to do huge things through you – yes, you! There is no limit to what you can accomplish through Him. Learn to see yourself correctly and change your story by not letting your past affect your future.

Go!

Now go, get off the couch and be awesome. This book has come to an end, but the principles you have learned are ones that must be applied daily.

Refer to this book often, read it again, bookmark chapters and reread them, and commit the principles to memory so you can remind yourself often how Jesus sees you and how you can deal with life when it seems impossible.

You are amazing! God has made you unique and gifted you in incredible ways. So, go. Go love, go shine, go give, go be selfless to a world that desperately needs to know that they, too, are amazing and there is a God who loves them unconditionally.

About The Author

As a pastor, author, speaker, and coach, Todd has a passion for reaching people for Christ and guiding them into a real relationship with Him. Over the last decade, Todd has devoted himself to raising up and empowering a generation of students to change the world for Christ. Todd is the founder of StokedOnYouthMinistry.com as well as a regular contributor, author, and speaker for various ministry companies.

Todd graduated from California Baptist University and currently serves as the Middle School Pastor at Cornerstone Fellowship Livermore. When he isn't writing, speaking, or putting on events for students, he plays and coaches baseball, watches any sport he can, and goes surfing as often as he can. His favorite role is that of husband to Rachael and dad to Carly, Cassy, Avery, and Ellie.

Connect With Todd:

Website: www.thetoddjones.com, www.stokedonyouthministry.com
Twitter: @TheTodd_Jones
Instagram: @TheTodd_Jones

Made in the USA
San Bernardino, CA
07 November 2018